FIRST HOME
decorating

Jill Blake

FIRST HOME
decorating

Jill Blake

The beginner's guide to creating a beautiful home

hamlyn

First published in Great Britain in 2004 by
Hamlyn, a division of Octopus Publishing Group Ltd
2–4 Heron Quays, London E14 4JP

Distributed in the United States and Canada by
Sterling Publishing Co., Inc.
387 Park Avenue South, New York, NY 10016-8810

ISBN 0 600 61045 4

A CIP catalogue record for this book is available from the British Library

Printed and bound in China

10 9 8 7 6 5 4 3 2 1

In describing all the projects in this book, every care has been taken
to recommend the safest methods of working. Before starting any
task, you should be confident that you know what you are doing, and
that you know how to use all tools and equipment safely.
   The Publishers cannot accept any legal responsibility or liability for
accidents or damage arising from the use of any items mentioned,
or in the carrying out of any of the projects described.

contents

introduction

It is an exciting moment when you finally receive the keys and open the front door to your first home. Almost immediately you will be thinking about how to decorate and furnish it to suit your particular lifestyle and personality. Your head will be full of colours, patterns and textures; ideas for floors and fabrics; plans for kitchens and bathrooms; and thoughts on everything from essential furniture to those all-important finishing touches.

Then comes the realization of how much there is to do to achieve the results you want. An older property may be in need of a complete revamp, from plumbing and electrical work to replastering, or it could be structurally sound, but in need of cosmetic changes and updating. If it is a new-build you may have been able to choose the basic surfaces and fittings, but will still want to stamp it with your own personality.

Whichever category your new home falls into, you will undoubtedly find this book helpful. It contains plenty of ideas on styles, colour and treatments for floors and walls, and shows you how to work a complete transformation on any room – without breaking the budget. There are step-by-step instructions for painting, papering and tiling, for sanding and laying floors, and all you require for specific projects, together with realistic advice on what you can do yourself, and when you should call in the experts.

Ideally, you should aim to live in a property for a year before you impose major changes. It is important to take the time to plan the space and furniture arrangements, so the rooms relate to their proposed purpose and function, and so that people will be able to move around comfortably. In this time you will also learn where you need hardwearing and easy-to-clean surfaces, where you can opt for more fragile, delicate materials and where thick, sound-absorbing textures might make an appreciable difference. Seeing how the light levels in different rooms change with the seasons can help you assess which rooms would benefit from visually warming up in winter or cooling down in summer, or from shiny, light-reflecting surfaces.

Before you rush out to buy so much as a paintbrush, it is also a good idea to take time to read the book through. Use the book to help you think about the style and ambience you would like to create. There are so many possibilities, but in a small property it is better to aim for continuity and use one style throughout. You may find it helpful to make up a sample board (see page 36), especially if you have existing items to incorporate.

If you do decide to do a lot of decorating, floor-laying and other do-it-yourself jobs, always plan things efficiently. Make sure you have sufficient materials to complete the project (this includes the right tools, adhesives and sealants, for example, as well as paint or fabric) and, especially, allow enough time. Trying to finish painting a ceiling at midnight, or papering an awkward wall with a heavily patterned design after a busy day at work is a recipe for disaster. Working in good light, at a pace that suits you, will give a much more satisfactory, professional-looking result.

Above all, however, enjoy turning your first house into a real home.

CHAPTER ONE

choosing the look

selecting a style

We all want our homes to be stylish and beautiful, but achieving that aim is not so easy.

There are so many variables, so many possibilities, that the choice can be bewildering.

Before you redecorate you should ideally try to live in a property for one year, to experience all the rooms at different times. This will also give you the time to research interior design and learn about the styles you like.

- Look at decoration with fresh eyes, for example in shops, hotels, restaurants, style museums and large houses open to the public, as well as in other people's homes.
- Books and magazines are a rich source of information and inspiration.
- Discover why some schemes are successful and others less so. Analyse colours, patterns, textures and forms. Note the way the space is used and lit (lighting is often an unappreciated aspect of decoration).
- Collect ideas such as features from magazines, pages from catalogues, pictures copied from books and samples of fabrics and paints.

the basic elements of a look

Colour creates ambience and can be used to visually alter the proportions of a room.

Pattern and texture help define the style; how they are mixed and matched can alter the entire effect.

Furniture immediately sets a room into context.

Window treatments give a room character, from heavy traditional drapes to streamlined blinds.

left Form and style can be added to a scheme with accessories – this table lamp helps to create a modern look.
centre A tessellated floor has a timeless elegance and could be used as a starting point on which to build a traditional theme.
right Cushions and throws provide texture and colour and can really change the 'feel' of a room.

sources of inspiration

inspiration from your surroundings

architecture does the room have interesting windows or a beautiful fireplace?

a cherished possession is there a special piece of furniture, a rug or a work of art that you could use as a starting point?

nature the seashore, a woodland in autumn or a butterfly's wing could all inspire a wonderful colour scheme.

inspiration from the past

georgian the hallmark of elegance. Well-proportioned rooms, subtle shades and fine furniture are indicative of Georgian style, although several styles or themes were popular during this era.

neoclassical ruled by symmetry. Architectural forms are echoed in furniture; classical and mythological detailing is a feature.

chinoiserie the perennial fascination of the East. Rich in lacquered furniture, bamboo, oriental porcelain and brilliant colours such as peacock blue, jade and imperial yellow.

regency a lighter successor to Georgian. Features include classic stripes, sprigged florals and pale, clear colours for walls and fabrics.

gothic a fanciful, recurring style that features pointed arches, carved wood, gilding and deep colours, especially in tapestries and hangings.

victorian a variety of styles spanning a long period. Typically much patterning and layering, velvets and overblown florals, swags and fringes, deep-buttoned chairs and solid, dark furniture.

arts and crafts a reaction to Victorian fussiness. Typified by simple stylized designs of flowers and foliage on wallpapers and fabrics and rustic, hand-crafted furniture. Shaker shares many of the same principles.

art nouveau a study in sinuosity. Distinctive organic forms are apparent from architecture to accessories. There are many interpretations, including Tiffany in the USA and Charles Rennie Macintosh's more geometric style.

above Streamlined Scandinavian style is comfortable and easy to live with; natural materials and wood are used on the main surfaces and colour is added in accessories.

art deco the look of the Jazz Age. Sleek, clean-cut forms and glossy textures combine with monochrome schemes.

bauhaus industrial design and materials developed for the home. Glass, chrome and plywood are imaginatively used with an emphasis on form and texture, rather than pattern.

1950s/60s 'the new modernity'. Furniture in fibreglass, plastic and metal, spindly or ovoid shapes and graphic or geometric patterns in primary and acid colours are typical of the era.

scandinavian fresh simplicity in natural materials. Pale woods and neutral colours sit with clean-lined, well-designed furniture.

Some of the most popular home-decorating styles are covered in some detail on the following pages.

country style

The feel is one of timelessness, of rooms that have seen generations come and go. The themes are rural –

animals, flowers, the countryside and country pursuits – and materials are natural rather than man-made.

Covering the simple, country cottage look and the rather grander, classical country house style, the emphasis here is on the comfortable and the lived-in – the country house style is often called 'shabby chic'. An open fireplace or woodburning stove would be a marvellous starting point for a country style.

furniture

Cottage-style furniture is rustic – benches, settles, rush-seated dining chairs and robust chests-of-drawers – made from light oak, pine or a fruit wood. Painted pieces can be distressed or decorated with stencils. Seating is comfortable – small sofas, an assortment of occasional chairs (some could be painted cane) – and may include a rocking chair. In the bedroom, the bed is likely to be wooden or metal-framed, with patchwork quilts and woollen throws. In the kitchen the cooking range has become synonymous with this style.

Country house furniture may have more style, but it is not fancy. Large rooms will take outsize wardrobes, large, solid dining tables and four-poster beds (house clearances and country auctions are a good source for this style).

floors

Stripped wooden boards suit the look well, strewn with rugs (plaited rag, hand-hooked or hand-tufted for the cottage look; faded oriental for the country house). Natural floorings, especially rush and seagrass matting, are also appropriate. Quarry tiles, slate or flagstones are good choices for kitchens, bathrooms and hallways.

window treatments

Keep the cottage look simple, with sill-length gathered curtains in printed cottons or woven checks, perhaps with a layer of cream lace or net beneath. Favourite fabrics include gingham, printed cottons (especially sprigged floral prints or mini-prints), tweeds, checks and perhaps some patchwork. Distressed wooden shutters would also be very appropriate. Curtains for a country-house style can be more elaborate, but pelmets and swags should not look too tailored. Soft velvets and large floral prints work well.

walls

Rough plaster, colourwashed or painted with matt distemper or emulsion paint, is an excellent backdrop for a cottage style. Pattern could come from borders or stencils and if using wallpaper choose a small-scale, unostentatious pattern. The walls of a country house would be less rustic, perhaps with some plaster moulding. Wood panelling is very typical.

above A country cottage living room has simple pine furniture, distempered walls and polished wooden floorboards. Texture and colour are added in tweed upholstery, blue and white china and gingham checks.

colours

Nothing too bright or primary: reds will be claret or rose rather than scarlet and yellows tend to old gold and primrose rather than egg. Neutrals will enhance the natural materials used and a few strong accents help emphasize important features.

accessories

Try decorated earthenware on dressers; wicker baskets; pewter and brass; patchwork and needlepoint cushions; lace or antique textiles; watercolours and prints and fresh-picked flowers.

above A painted armoire is used to store clothes and linen in a country-style bedroom. **right** Rag rugs, quilted covers, assorted cushions and simple curtains complete the country look.

contemporary urban style

Metal girders, roof trusses and steel or brick pillars may all be left exposed as part of this style, which is often associated with conversions of warehouses, factories or other industrial buildings. The look can also be applied to modern barn conversions and new-build country properties for a light, spacious, uncluttered interior.

Typically, the contemporary urban living space is open-plan and fluid, so planning the use of space is important, as is unity of design between different areas. Capacious storage is vital as this is not a style that makes a virtue out of everyday mess or eclectic collections, although the inner workings of modern technology are often proudly on view.

furniture

The look is sleek and streamlined, with individual pieces making a statement – they may even be an art form in their own right. Chairs are often metal-framed, and leather, linen or tweed are favoured for upholstery. This type of interior may incorporate a few older pieces, even antiques, which should be used as a bold focal point, and be cleverly lit.

floors

Original wide wooden boards suit the style, but so does cement or concrete, which can be painted, coloured or polished. For a softer feel, cover floors with studded rubber, inlaid designs in linoleum or vinyl, metal (or metal-look) tiles, leather or a glittery vinyl. Walkways and interior stairs might be a combination of metal and glass. Carpets are definitely not part of this look, although a 'designer' rug or a faux animal skin could add a softer texture.

window treatments

This type of interior does not have conventional curtains. If they are well shaped, windows may be left unadorned, or they can be screened with blinds, shutters or sheer fabric drapes, which filter the light.

walls

Walls are always plain – wallpaper is definitely not an option – but they may be boldly coloured. Exposed brickwork can be left untreated. Other wall treatments that work well include paint (perhaps with a metallic finish), plywood or laminated panels and polished plaster. A panel of glass bricks lets in light and adds textural interest.

colours

Colours are usually neutral, especially in main living areas. Particularly suitable are the rather stark 'true' neutrals of black, white and grey, combined with silver-coloured metals. Slightly softer are the broken whites, creams and beiges, warm taupes and browns. Bright flashes of colour can be added in accents to enliven the scheme, and often the bathroom and kitchen areas are strongly coloured with bright blues, aquas and emeralds or bold orange, purple and yellow.

accessories

Stand-alone accessories in bold, dramatic shapes or unusual textures are typical and groups should present a sense of unity, such as three single blooms each in identical tall glass vases. Eye-catching art, from a fabric wall-hanging to an acrylic painting, look dramatic against plain walls, and architectural plants – palms, ferns, topiary – are perfect. Lighting for emphasis is important.

above Exposed brickwork adds texture to a contemporary bedroom. Venetian blinds diffuse the light and the blue and white bedding adds a touch of soft colour and texture.

previous page Simple furniture and plain painted walls create an uncluttered look in an open-plan living area, and light fittings make their own statement.

eclectic style

The best interior designs have always drawn inspiration from different countries and cultures

to add richness and excitement, and eclectic describes a highly original, slightly bohemian look.

This rather unstructured and personal style does need a deft touch to succeed. The cosy, intimate atmosphere works particularly well in bedrooms, dining rooms, studio apartments and one-room living. Reclamation can play an important part – either the restoration of an existing feature or discovering the right architectural detail in a salvage yard. Recycled materials, such as driftwood and metal, can work as accessories.

furniture

With no single period or look to follow, furniture can be in assorted shapes and styles and local house clearance auctions or junk shops are fruitful hunting areas. Veranda and conservatory furniture in cane, wicker, bamboo and cast iron are often used in sitting rooms and dining rooms. Continue this sub-tropical/colonial feel with open-work screens (used to divide the space or conceal clutter), rattan blinds and perhaps a traditional mosquito net (dyed a vivid colour) over the bed. Painting disparate items the same colour will integrate them into the overall scheme, and throws and embroidered or antique textiles and animal prints can disguise slightly battered pieces.

floors

Floorboards can be bleached, scrubbed, stained or painted. Any natural flooring is good, such as stone, slate, brick, terracotta tiles or, for a softer feel underfoot, a woven floorcovering such as sisal, seagrass or rush matting. An interesting alternative, if you have an artistic bent, is a painted floorcloth. Add colour and cosiness with a selection of rugs in ethnic weaves or perhaps animal print.

window treatments

Window treatments should incorporate layers of pattern and colour. Combine wooden venetian, rattan or fabric blinds with heavily textured or richly patterned over-curtains. Team a pierced screen (suggestive of a Turkish harem) with a sheer drape in muslin or an exotic sari fabric. Rather than a conventional pelmet, a lambrequin, with its exaggerated side panels, provides an interesting, different look.

walls

There is no need for monochrome restraint. Walls can be papered, perhaps in panels, covered with fabric or an unusual texture such as grasscloth or hessian, or painted. They could be highly decorative, with a collage or even a mural. Paisley, ikat, flame-stitch and swirling geometrics are all patterns that work well, and a bold, plain colour can be enhanced with a patterned border on both walls and fabrics. Tiling in bathrooms and kitchens should be anything but clinical. Intricate geometric patterns or mosaics give an Indian or North African feel, or use plain tiles in different colours to create a patchwork effect.

colours

Colour can draw together a mix of styles and patterns into a cohesive whole. Favoured colours are strong and earthy – terracotta, ochre, Indian red – or the brilliant hues of oriental silks – peacock, turquoise, lacquer red, purple. Combine them with natural textures in neutral colours for a slightly calmer look.

right The warm Indian-red bedcover and walls help to unify an eclectic mix in a bedroom, where luggage and hat boxes are used for storage.

accessories

An important element of the eclectic style. Open shelves displaying books, china, glassware, personal collections and mementoes set the scene. Cushions can be covered in an assortment of fabrics and trims and subtle, dimmable lighting (including lamps and candles) is preferable. Plants, rather than cut flowers, are ideal, such as pots of herbs in the kitchen, wicker containers of steam-loving plants in the bathroom and larger palms and 'jungly' plants in the living room.

left A conservatory feel is created in a living room, with wrought-iron and rattan furniture. 'Jungle prints' are combined with simple florals and a mish-mash of accessories to create an eclectic look.

the personal touch

Interior design is now as much a fashion industry as the garment trade, and trends come and go just as quickly. Be wary of adopting the latest fad, as it can soon look dated – choose a style which will suit the function of the room and your particular lifestyle, as well as reflecting your taste.

mixing styles

There is no reason why you couldn't successfully have an Art Deco bedroom and bathroom, a country cottage kitchen, a romantic Regency dining room and an ethnic theme in a conservatory, but

take care that this does not result in a disjointed effect, each detracting from the other. One way to do this is to create visual links. Colour will be your greatest ally here, as tones of similar colour flowing from room to room will help unify the whole.

Don't lose sight of the room's function either. Over-fussy styles don't often work in kitchens or home offices, for example, and a minimalist, all-white scheme may be inappropriate for a multi-purpose family living room.

left A decorative mirror frame adds a highly personal touch to a dressing table – the lustrous texture is echoed in the string of pearls.

I've chosen a style – now what?

From the ideas and samples you have collected, pick out those that fit your theme. Spread them out on a sheet of white paper or card, adding and subtracting from the mix until you have compiled an 'ideas' or 'mood' board. Keep this for a few days in 'its' room, getting opinions from others and making further notes. This will help you compile your sample board (see page 36).

Once you have a clear idea of how the room will look, you can start planning the detail and the practicalities.

below Glass and metal, sea shells collected on various holidays or an antique appliquéd fabric can all help to personalize a scheme.

CHAPTER TWO

colour

understanding colour

Colour is the most powerful decorating tool of all. It creates mood, atmosphere and impact and is usually the first thing we notice about a room. It can be used to stimulate and to relax, and can bring a touch of sunshine into a dark, dismal area.

Some things to remember about colour:

- Colour is affected by light: consider your chosen colours by natural daylight at different times of the day, and also by the room's lighting.

- The amount of colour used affects its apparent intensity, so try to see a colour on the scale at which it will be used to judge its impact.

- Texture affects how we see colour: a rough, bobbly fabric will appear different from a light-reflecting gloss paint in a matching hue.

- Our perception of colour is affected by neighbouring colours (see page 28). A small red and white print, for instance, will appear pink from a short distance away.

- Neutrals are an invaluable addition to the palette (see page 30). Use them to provide harmony or to tone down a strong scheme.

left Fresh cool greens create an impression of space, especially when combined with neutrals such as white and cream.

the colour wheel

A colour wheel shows how the spectrum of colours turns full circle, each colour graduating into the next. The colour wheel is made up of:

primary colours red, yellow and blue. These cannot be obtained by mixing.

secondary colours obtained by mixing two primary colours: orange (red and yellow), green (yellow and blue) and violet (blue and red).

tertiary colours mixes of a primary and a neighbouring secondary (blue-green, orange-red, for example).

The infinite subtleties of colours are obtained by the addition of black, grey and white, which do not feature on the colour wheel in their own right since they are not, strictly speaking, colours at all, but an absence or saturation of light.

You will find colours referred to indiscriminately as hues, tints and shades, but these actually have specific meanings:

hues are pure colours, without the addition of neutrals.

tints are hues with varying degrees of white added.

shades are obtained by adding black to a hue.

tones, sometimes called mid-tones, result from the addition of grey.

The colours on the red side of the wheel are considered warm and appear to advance towards you, while colours on the blue side are cool, or receding, and can make a space look larger (although a strong blue can be enclosing). The warmth or coolness of a mixed colour varies greatly with the predominance of the hue used in the mix – some greens can be warm, if there is more yellow in them, or cool if there is more blue, for example.

The following pages explore the qualities of primary and secondary colours, in all their tints, shades and tones.

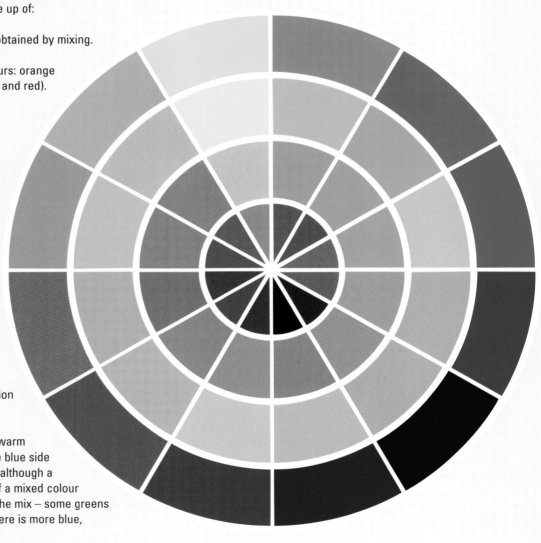

reds, oranges and yellows

These warm colours will make a room seem cosy and intimate but, if the colour values are too strong or bright,

the result can be overpowering, almost claustrophobic.

red

Red is the colour of vitality and energy – it is bright, exciting and dramatic. As it is also the strongest advancing colour it can be overpowering and will make a room seem smaller if the stronger hues are used. The strength of its warmth works well in cold bathrooms and kitchens, and, because it is a welcoming colour, it is good for halls. Red is also an appetite-inducing colour, and because it makes food (especially meat) look appetizing it has long been a favourite choice for the dining room.

When red is tinted, it becomes pink – a feminine colour, associated with love and romance. Pastel pinks and deeper rose will help you to create a really romantic bedroom. A hint of blue in the pink will turn it a pinky-mauve, a mysterious, sophisticated colour, ideal for bedrooms and bathrooms. Deeper tones and shades of red are more subtle, such as rose, plum and claret. These create an elegant look in traditional sitting rooms, hallways, dining rooms or studies.

orange

Orange is almost as strong and advancing as red, and can be used in a similar way. It can be highly stimulating, especially if combined with black or grey, white, or with its complementary colour, blue. These are combinations that can work very successfully in children's playrooms, bathrooms and kitchens.

Tinted oranges become peach, coral or apricot, delicate, feminine and romantic colours that work well in bedrooms. When it is greyed down, orange becomes terracotta, tan or chestnut brown, producing very versatile decorating colours that can be used with white or cream to create an elegant, warm, inviting scheme for a hall, living room or home office.

yellow

Yellow is a joyful colour associated with sunshine, warmth and summer. It is also the colour of the mind, intellect and creative energy. Bright yellow will bring light and sunshine into the darkest room, but as it is highly stimulating, use with care. Neutral backgrounds, and the classical Scandinavian mix of yellow with blue, will help to ensure it is not overpowering. Yellow is a good colour for children's rooms, hallways and bathrooms.

Greyed yellow becomes mustard, rich gold or subtle honey brown. These are the colours to use in sophisticated schemes for more traditional drawing rooms, bedrooms and studies. A yellow with a hint of olive green can be elegant – but take care as it can look grey under artificial light. Pale yellow has a highly reflective quality and will make a small space seem larger and brighter. When it goes towards green it becomes lime, which can be stimulating and is a good accent colour.

left Red and yellow, used together, create a feeling of heat and sunshine. Adding a cool contrast – here in the form of a green pot – will emphasize the warmth. **right** Different values of one colour work well with a tonal contrast. Here, yellow has been combined successfully with neutral off-whites to create a fresh sitting room.

greens, blues and violets

Colours on the cooler side of the colour wheel often appear far from cold. Many of them mix easily together and there are fewer strident colours, making them a 'safe' choice on which to base a scheme.

green

Green is the 'balance' colour, halfway between the warm and cool colours of the spectrum. It is the colour of nature and guaranteed to suggest 'landscape', so is a good choice for a city apartment or dull townhouse. However, green can be very cold, especially if it has blue undertones, but mixes well with contrasting warm colours to ward off the chill.

Pale tints of green will create a very spacious look for small bathrooms and bedrooms, and when green goes towards blue it becomes minty, which is very refreshing in a kitchen.

Dark shades of green are rich and sophisticated: deep malachite or forest green work well with both traditional and modern styles.

Greyed values of green can be very subtle. Sage and olive greens are very elegant, and look good in country-style drawing rooms, classic hallways or modern dining rooms, but, like yellow-greens, need to be well lit to ensure they don't look gloomy at night.

left Pale blues and greens help to create a calm and relaxing mood. These colours are ideal for rooms intended for relaxation, such as a bedroom or a bathroom.

blue

Blue is the colour of harmony, peace and devotion. It is associated with the sky and wide vistas, and will create an impression of space. But as it is basically a cool colour, use it with care. Blue is fairly low in reflective value, and will diffuse and soften strong sunlight, calming down over-bright rooms. However, clear, bright blue can also be very cheerful, which makes it ideal for children's rooms, an urban sitting room or a basement kitchen.

The pure values of blue, especially as it starts to go towards green – peacock, turquoise – can be very demanding, so use these in small amounts if the room is small. Lightened to aqua, its freshness works well in bathrooms and kitchens.

The greyed tones and shades of blue can be subtle, but they can also be dull if not lit very carefully. They can look very effective teamed with crisp neutrals – white or cream – or warmed up with contrasting accents of orange, yellow or bright pink.

violet

In its strongest value, a regal purple, this is a vibrant and demanding colour that needs neutral contrasts. It works particularly well with its adjacent colours on the wheel: blue, blue-green and pink-violet.

The pale tints of lilac and lavender are delicate and feminine, giving a romantic feel to a bedroom or bathroom, or a sophisticated look to a sitting room.

Greyed lighter tints give subtle heathers that are changeable in different lights, while the darker shades yield rich plums and aubergines. These work well in period settings, teamed with golds, cream and pale yellow in parlours or dining rooms.

right Using several shades of blue gives this bathroom a dramatic look. Teamed with neutral grey and white adds emphasis.

using harmonious and contrasting colours

The colour wheel is an invaluable tool. It illustrates the natural complements and contrasts of each colour, and is a ready reminder of how colours relate to each other. Use it as a guide to which colours work well together and to inspire unusual combinations.

harmonious colours

Harmonious colours are neighbours on the colour wheel and together they will create a relaxing atmosphere. A tighter variation on this is to work within a single colour, from its lightest tint to darkest shade, but without straying sideways into the next segment of the colour wheel. This results in a monochromatic scheme, and will also provide a calm, easy-to-live-with ambience.

building up a monochromatic scheme

Use paint colour cards as a guide – these are easy to pick up at paint stockists. There will probably be several cards to cover all the possibilities within a single colour, giving you a wide range to play with. You might use the palest value of the colour for the woodwork, a slightly stronger tint for the ceiling, a mid-tone for the walls and a deeper shade for the floor covering. Also look out for papers and fabrics that use different tones of the same colour.

You will find most monochromatic schemes need brightening up with accent colours – look back at the colour wheel to see which hues contrast with your chosen colour.

right Harmonious, or related, colours can be striking. Blue-violet and red-violet have been used here to dramatic effect.

contrasting colours

Contrasting or complementary colours are opposites on the wheel: red and green; yellow and violet; blue and orange. By choosing contrasting colours, you are automatically teaming a warm colour with a cool one. If you focus on a strong hue of a warm colour (red, for example) for a minute or so then look away, you will see an 'after colour' of its opposite (green) – the eye plays strange tricks!

When used together, contrasting colours can be stimulating and exciting, but if the colour values of both are too bright the effect can be disturbing. However, contrasts include the colours in all their tints, tones and shades – so a scheme based on sugar pink and olive green or turquoise and terracotta will still be contrasting but not overpowering. Such 'diluted' contrasts work well in rooms where you don't want to relax too much, but don't want to be continually stimulated either.

A contrasting colour scheme can also be split-complementary, by using a primary colour combined with the two tertiary colours that flank its opposite – such as blue with red-orange and yellow-orange.

You can create an equally successful contrasting colour scheme without actually using direct opposites, as long as you combine warm and cool colours, for example, blue with yellow, orange with jade-green or green with violet.

right Contrasting colours do not have to be strong –
they can be a subtle variation on the original hue.
The opposites of heather (purple) and deep gold
(yellow) complement each other in this dining room.

working with neutrals

The only three true neutrals are white, black and the in-between of grey, but there are also the accepted neutrals
– or naturals – the broken whites, creams, beiges, taupes and soft browns of stone, wood, undyed linen or wool.

Neutrals on their own create a harmonious scheme, and are often effective for a very contemporary look, but they can be difficult to keep clean. A basic rule of interior design is to consider the practical alongside the aesthetic. It would be impractical, for example, to decorate a hallway in pale creams with an off-white carpet and expect it to cope with a regular flow of visitors, muddy feet and even bike or baby-buggy wheels. On the other hand, a scheme like this would give a pleasing atmosphere of calm in a main bedroom.

Black and white, especially if used to create a bold pattern, is the most stimulating and disturbing of combinations, and needs to be used with care.

adding accent colours

Accents can be added in accessories, but also introduced in a patterned fabric, wallpaper or flooring. The dominant colour in a pattern should relate to the main scheme, with secondary colours echoed in other plain accessories.

To vary the tonal balance, add warm accents to a cool scheme, cool ones to a warm scheme and strong, rich colours to neutrals.

Ways to introduce accent colours into a sitting room or dining room:

- cushions or padded seat covers
- rugs
- plants and flowers
- pictures, prints and photographs (including interesting frames)
- glass or china
- lamp bases and shades
- table covers
- candles and holders

In the kitchen:

- pots and pans
- china, pottery and glass
- tea towels, aprons and oven gloves
- pictures
- herbs in decorative pots

In the bathroom:

- towels and bath mats
- boxes and baskets for toiletries
- pictures
- plants

In the bedroom:

- bedside lamps and shades
- pictures
- rugs
- cushions and throws

Note: bedlinen should be chosen as an integral part of the scheme and not as an accessory.

left A neutral kitchen with a natural wood floor can be made more interesting with colourful accessories, plants and interesting textures.

neutrals in a mixed scheme

On their own, neutrals can be rather boring, so it is a good idea to enliven them with contrasting accents (see box opposite). Follow the basic rule of relating these accents to the overall style of the room, and choose warm or cool colours according to the atmosphere you want. With a predominantly neutral scheme you could use several different accent colours, mixing cool and warm, or different tonal values of one or two colours.

Neutrals can also make a major contribution to other colour schemes. They form a good background to printed fabrics and wallcoverings, and provide an element of quiet contrast, often unnoticed.

when is white not white?

Many so-called neutrals, especially near-whites, are actually very pale tints of a 'proper' colour. Creams can have hints of yellow or pink while 'greiges' (grey/beige) and browns can have undertones of warm orange or cool blue. These origins may not be apparent until placed near another colour or neutral. Pure white woodwork can make an off-white carpet look dirty, and a subtly shaded tweed fabric can just appear grey in the wrong company.

left Subtle colour accents in pink and brown add interest to this neutral living-room scheme based on creams and whites.

visual tricks with colour

As well as creating an atmosphere with colour, and visually heating or cooling a room, you can use colour, pattern and light to play decorating 'tricks' that appear to alter proportions – far less expensive than any structural alteration.

to lower a ceiling

- Paint it a warm, advancing colour and colour the walls with a cool contrast.
- Colour the floor to match the ceiling, or use the same tonal value for both.
- Team a brilliant white ceiling with dark walls (white ceilings do not always look taller).
- Use a horizontal pattern on the walls, or divide them up with a dado rail and picture rail or frieze.
- Paint the cornice/coving to contrast with the ceiling.
- Tent the ceiling with fabric.
- Tall items of furniture will make a room look lower.

to add height to a low room

- Paint the ceiling a pale receding colour – sky blue is particularly effective.
- Colour the ceiling a slightly lighter tone than the walls or match it to the background of any wallcovering.
- Use a light-reflecting texture on the ceiling but only if the plasterwork is good.
- Use a bold, vertical treatment on the walls.
- Use the same mini-print pattern over walls and ceiling making sure the pattern is non-directional.
- Furnish the room with low-slung furniture.

dealing with ceilings and beams

- To hide beams, girders, slopes and angles, colour them all to match the walls and ceiling; to make these features stand out, treat them in a contrasting colour.

to make a small room look larger

- Use pale receding colours and small patterns.
- Avoid too much contrast in colour.
- Use light-reflecting textures on main surfaces.
- Choose a harmonious, neutral or monochromatic colour scheme.
- Use mirrors to reflect light.

to make a large room cosier

- Use warm, advancing colours and contrasting textures.
- Use bold patterns on the main surfaces.
- Use complementary colours, such as curtains to contrast with walls and furniture that contrasts with the floor.
- Emphasize different features or areas with lighting.

to camouflage ugly features

- Paint or colour unsightly features the same colour as the background. This is particularly effective with radiators.
- Use receding colours on both the feature and the background.

right Voile panels are used to filter the daylight in a pale-toned bedroom scheme.

to enhance attractive features

- Paint or colour attractive features to contrast with the background, for example use neutral colours against a white background or an advancing colour against a receding one.

- Light features dramatically.

to make a narrow area look wider

- Paint or paper end walls in a bold, advancing colour or with a strong pattern.

- Dress a window in an end wall with floor-to-ceiling/wall-to-wall curtains in a companion fabric to the wall treatment.

- Put a well-lit, eye-catching piece of art or group of pictures on an end wall.

- Paint or paper both long walls in a cool, receding colour.

- Hang mirrors on one of the long walls.

- Make the floor seem wider with widthwise stripes or a chequerboard effect, and paint the skirting to match the floor.

to make a box room less square

- Create a focal point in the centre of one wall, such as a fireplace, opulent window treatment or bold drapes above a bed to contrast with the surrounding wall.

- Colour one wall in a bold contrast to the other walls.

- Use one wall for built-in furniture, decorated with contrasting panels or beading.

- Create a trompe l'oeil effect on one wall.

right A neutral colour scheme has been chosen to make this living room appear larger, with textural contrast added in fabrics and a rug.

creating a colour scheme

Good colour schemes don't just happen. They have to be planned, and, as nobody can 'carry colour' successfully in their eye, this means doing some accurate colour-matching. The best way to do this is to take samples of decorating materials home and look at them in the room in which you intend to use them, under both daylight and artificial light.

working with what you've got

In an ideal world, you would be able to create a colour scheme with absolutely no constraints at all. But in reality, most of us have to work a new colour scheme around an existing item such as a bathroom suite, kitchen units or a sofa.

All rooms have existing features that could be used as the starting-off point for a colour scheme.

architectural style this can suggest an overall style for the room, and any interesting features should be enhanced. An attractive fireplace is worth emphasizing, so the chimney breast can be coloured a rich dark tone to 'bring forward' a light-coloured fire surround, or painted a pale colour to contrast with a dark surround. If the room has beautiful windows, give them a very simple treatment to enhance their natural shape.

the orientation of the room and the daylight it gets. For rooms without much morning light, choose colours from the warmer side of the colour spectrum. For those bathed in morning sunlight, which are cooler and darker in the evening, try to work with the paler 'sunshine' tones. Rooms that are bright and warm from midday onwards work best with cooler, receding colours.

room size small rooms can feel claustrophobic if strong colours are used. It is usually better to use pale, cool colours – blues, greens, lilacs – or neutral schemes to suggest a larger space. It also helps to include some shiny textures and mirrors to reflect the light and make the room seem bigger. If you are dealing with a very large space, use strong, contrasting colours and even bold pattern, to create a more cosy effect.

left The strong, warm colour of the chimney breast emphasizes the simple fire surround – a useful visual trick to make a square room look more interesting.

balancing colours and patterns

It is important to relate the strength of colours and size of pattern to the scale on which they will be used. Bright colours and bold, jazzy patterns will look at least twice as strong on a large expanse of floor or wall, so always try to see as large a sample as possible. If you plan to paint a wall, do a test on a length of lining paper and pin it up in the room for a few days.

Small patterns produce a quite different effect when seen on a large scale, so don't judge them from a small swatch. Some mini-prints lose all definition and give the impression of a texture, rather than a distinct pattern when applied to the whole wall.

Combining patterns is one of the trickiest schemes to pull off successfully. Use a sample board (see page 36) to experiment with different effects. It is often too broad a colour range that makes pattern mixes look messy, so study carefully the colours that make up each design and aim for patterns that share a common palette.

Don't overlook the important part neutrals play in the balance of an overall scheme. Even a rich, colourful scheme will rely on white or cream for contrast, to emphasize the brilliance of the other colours and to avoid sensory overload.

right Neutral colours provide a calm background, which can then be enhanced with strong colours and interesting textures to create a modern, eclectic look.

'Good colour schemes don't just happen – they have to be planned'

sample board success

Creating a sample board is an excellent way to plan your colour scheme and avoid costly mistakes. Collect samples of the materials you plan to use and see how they look when laid out next to each other on a board. Include colours from paint charts, swatches of furnishing and curtain fabrics, pieces of wallcoverings and samples of carpets. Make sure that the materials are more or less in the correct proportion (for example, wall and floor samples will be larger than the upholstery or curtain fabric).

how it's done

The starting point for this board is the rug (15). This is striped in golds, greens, yellows and terracottas and will be placed on a wooden floor in a sitting room. It is the centrepiece around which the rest of the sample board is put together.

the scheme begins to take shape

wallcoverings the main wallcovering is soft yellow-green, with a bolder texture and deeper colour on a grasscloth for the chimney breast to enhance the modern fireplace. A paler yellow-green paint has been selected for the ceiling.

soft window treatments a silky, textured fabric for curtains is added in a darker tone than the walls, but of a similar colour, to enrich without distracting.

additional window treatment rattan blinds have been chosen to go under the curtains, providing privacy and filtering the light.

upholstery upholstery fabrics in contrasting textures in green, gold and terracotta complete the theme. The tweedy texture for the sofa cover contains some turquoise, which could be used, with terracotta, for extra accessories.

decorative elements paintings or prints can be introduced at the final stage to pull together all the elements of the design, including any accent colours.

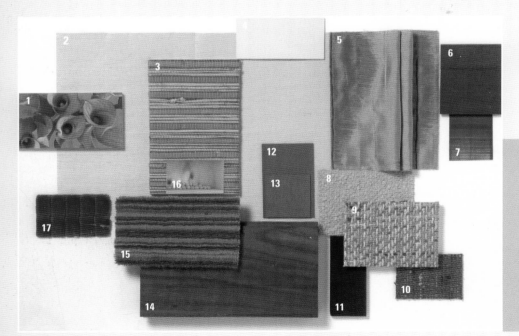

elements of a sample board

1	picture	9	sofa 2 fabric
2	main wallcovering	10	single chair fabric
3	wallcovering for chimney breast	11	wood sample for shelving
4	ceiling paint	12	tub chair 1
5	curtain fabric	13	tub chair 2
6	blinds: wood type	14	wood flooring sample
7	blinds: overall look	15	rug sample
8	sofa 1 fabric	16	contemporary fireplace
		17	cushion fabric

CHAPTER THREE

paint, paper and tiles

wall treatments

Walls are usually the dominant aspect of a room, so the treatment you choose will set the overall look.

As well as choosing a good look you will need to decide what will work best in practical terms.

first, consider the basics

Are the walls in good condition, or is the plaster flaking? Is damp a problem? Do they need insulating? Covering up problems is usually a waste of money and effort, as the end result will never look satisfactory and any serious defects, such as damp, will soon ruin the new decorations. So make sure you right any wrongs before you start decorating, and for structural problems, call in the experts.

What will the room be used for? It is important to consider the practicality of the wall treatment. For example, the walls of bathrooms and kitchens need to be spongeable and resistant to moisture. Halls and stairs often become scuffed and finger-marked, so these should also have a hard-wearing, easy-to-clean surface.

using professionals

For some jobs, such as hanging a difficult-to-handle wallpaper or painting a towering stairwell, you might want to call in a professional decorator. Get at least three estimates from recommended professionals and ask for an idea of the time it will take as well as the cost. Make sure you are comparing like with like: some tradespeople estimate to supply and fix, while others quote for doing the work only, and expect you to supply the materials.

disguising a sound but ugly wall

A structurally sound wall with a few minor but unsightly imperfections can be treated and the imperfections disguised. Avoid using a finish with a shine to it, as this will magnify any imperfections in the plasterwork. It is sometimes possible to camouflage uneven plaster or ugly tiles with wood-cladding, laminate or even fabric. Existing tiles, if they are firm, can be over-tiled or repainted.

wallcoverings: the options

paint usually the most economical choice. Paint can be matched to almost any shade imaginable, and you can create special effects with it, from basic colourwashing to murals and trompe-l'oeil (see pages 42–44).

wallpaper there is an endless range of wallpaper styles, including interesting textured papers, designs with matching or complementary fabrics, and period patterns. The prices also vary widely and some papers are more straightforward to hang than others (see pages 46–51).

tiles the conventional answer for 'wet' areas, but practical anywhere where a tough, washable surface is required. The choice of tiles is not limited to ceramic (see pages 52–60).

laminate panels often used where the surface needs to be impervious to water. Laminate comes in almost any pattern, colour or texture, but marble and tile effects are popular. The panels can be fixed on battens or, if the wall is perfectly smooth, stuck in place with impact adhesive.

wood cladding tongue-and-groove cladding 'secret-nailed' to battens is not too difficult for a competent amateur to put up. The wood can be oiled, waxed, stained or painted, but remember to do a colour test on a spare piece of wood first, as colours can vary from the shade card.

fabric hessian (burlap), silk, linen, felt and other fabrics can be bonded to a paper backing and hung like wallpaper. Unbacked fabric can be stretched in place over battens. Both are jobs for an expert.

luxury wallcoverings it is easy to be seduced by luxury wallcoverings such as grasscloth and leather, but bear in mind they are expensive, difficult to hang and may be vulnerable.

left Pattern interest can be added to walls using plain paint. Bold harmonious or contrasting coloured squares look stunning, as illustrated in this living room.
right Freehand-painted or stencilled patterns will create an individual look. Here the walls and fabric have been coordinated, with the fabric design echoed on the wall.

choosing paint

There are many different types of paint available today, designed to meet all the requirements of the home decorator. From paints that cover in one coat to paints that create specialist effects.

types of paint
Most paints fall into the following categories:
water-based dries quickly and without a strong solvent smell. Water-based paints include emulsion, distemper and water-based gloss.

oil-based slower drying but provides a harder finish. Oil-based paints include eggshell, gloss and enamel.

aerosol spray mostly for metal (such as radiators) or large stencil designs. Aerosol sprays can be matt or metallic.

organic free of solvents or other harmful chemicals, organic paints are biodegradable and allow walls to breathe.

The label on the paint can will tell you whether the paint is water- or oil- (solvent-) based. Here is where you will also find information on its recommended uses and, most importantly, covering power. Remember that you cannot use a water-based paint over an oil-based one.

finishes
matt finishes matt emulsions have an attractive, sometimes chalky look. A 'dead flat' oil-based paint is often chosen for an authentic period look for wood.

mid-sheen finishes mid-sheen emulsions are spongeable. Mid-sheen oil-based paints, also labelled 'satinwood' or 'satin sheen', have a less 'hard' look than gloss.

gloss finishes are generally used for a tough, washable surface on wood and metal, but you can also buy metallic emulsion for walls and ceilings. The light-reflective quality will magnify any surface faults.

eggshell finishes are often used for woodwork and by specialist decorative paint finishers, as a base for a painted technique combining glazes. The eggshell finish has a subtle sheen, like an egg, and although it is not as tough as a gloss finish, can be washed to remove sticky finger marks.

metallic finishes can be used on wood and radiators. There are also special paints formulated to use on domestic appliances such as refrigerators, to give them a new lease of life. Some metallic emulsion paints can be used on walls and ceilings.

polished finishes are currently in vogue and have a smooth, lustrous look, without being too shiny. The application of polished plaster is a job for the expert.

textured finishes can be used on walls and ceilings, especially if the original surface is poor. Some paints come with 'additives' and can be painted on with a brush or roller to create a 'rough cast' effect. Others may be textured with special tools. Most textured finishes are very difficult to remove, so if you want to be able to change the décor frequently, it might be wiser to hang a textured wallcovering and paint over it with emulsion paint – it can then be removed, using a steam-stripper, if necessary.

calculating quantities
To calculate how much paint you will need, just measure the walls – height and length – and multiply to give you the area to be covered. There is no need to deduct areas of windows or doors. Paint-can labels will suggest an average coverage, but highly textured or very porous walls may be very 'thirsty', so double the quantity. You will need more paint to cover a dark colour than if you are painting a light surface with a similar or darker colour.

Always buy sufficient paint and ensure it comes from the same mixing – you can do this by checking the batch number on the can. Colour can vary subtly but noticeably between batches.

essential preparation

*Whatever you do, don't paint an unprepared surface. Drastic preparation work isn't always necessary,
but the area must be clean, smooth and dry otherwise the paint may not adhere or last very long.*

walls

Walls in good condition may only need washing down, using sugar soap or another strong degreasing agent. Scrape away any loose plaster and fill small holes and cracks with a proprietary filler and sand down. Large holes may need replastering. Give new plaster time to dry out.

To strip off old paper (see page 51), work on one wall at a time. A hired steam stripper will make this work easier. Once stripped, seal the walls with a watery solution of wallpaper adhesive and leave overnight. Rub and wipe away dust with a damp sponge.

Lining paper (see page 46) applied to a wall before painting will improve the surface and mask any minor imperfections, giving a better final result.

wood

Sound, previously painted wood will just need a wash down and light sanding to give the new paint a 'key' to adhere to. Remove flaking paint or varnish with a hot air stripper (take care not to singe the wood) or chemical stripper. Cut out and replace damaged wood, then sand the entire surface in the direction of the grain. Wash oily woods with solvent.

On bare wood, use a primer first. Quick-drying acrylic is suitable for most purposes, but use an oil-based primer for areas of heavy wear. Once dry, apply an undercoat (two coats for extra coverage). Lightly sand down between coats and remove all dust.

metal

Rub down previously painted metal with emery paper. Remove rust with a wire brush and use a filler (for car bodywork) to fill chips and dents. Apply a coat of metal primer. Unpainted metal should only need cleaning and priming (radiators often come ready-primed). Follow with an undercoat.

left Always test paint colours before applying them to the walls, ceiling or woodwork. To do this you can paint a small piece of wood or lining paper.

how to paint

You can use paint for uninterrupted colour or to create stunning visual effects, from bold geometric patterning to delicate stencilling or a unique mural.

before you start

Ensure the walls are clean and dry (see page 43) and woodwork is prepared. Make sure you have the right tools and equipment close at hand, and enough paint to complete the job. It is a good idea to check that the paint comes from the same mixing (batch number) to avoid any difference in colour or tone from tin to tin.

safety note

A scaffold board supported by two ladders is safer than a single ladder, especially when painting a ceiling. For decorating a stairwell you will need to build a sturdy platform or, even better, hire a scaffold tower.

tools

- brushes in various sizes: 1–5cm (½–2 in) for edges and windows; up to 15 cm (6 in) for walls
- rollers, as an alternative to brushes for large areas. Suit the roller to the type of paint – textured paint needs a deep-pile roller. A small roller on a long handle is indispensable for reaching behind radiators
- paint pads: easy to use but not suitable for textured surfaces
- paint tray (when using roller or pads)
- protective sheets, old rags and newspapers
- masking tape or a paint shield
- paint stirrer
- paint kettle (optional, but sometimes easier than painting direct from the can)
- brush cleaner suited to the type of paint

walls and ceilings

When painting walls and ceilings remember to allow yourself enough time to complete the work. You can do one wall at a time, but you must paint the whole ceiling in one go.

1 Start to paint a ceiling in the corner nearest the window, and work away from the light. For a wall, try to start with one that is unbroken, and begin in a top corner.

2 Dip no more than one third of the bristles in the paint and wipe off the excess (string or thin wire tied across the top of the can or paint kettle is useful for this).

3 Begin around the edges with a small cutting-in brush, then change to a larger brush or roller – work across and down in strips about 75 cm (2 ft) wide, 'feathering' the edges so they blend invisibly. When using a roller, only part-fill the paint tray and don't overload the roller. Work with criss-cross strokes sideways and downwards, keeping the roller on the surface until almost dry (or you will get splashing).

order of work

It is important to follow the correct sequence when painting a room to avoid spoiling newly-painted surfaces and having to repaint them.

1	ceilings	4	windows
2	walls	5	radiators
3	doors	6	skirting boards (baseboards)

woodwork and metal

- Remove any window catches or handles and ensure radiators are cool.
- Don't be tempted to use too wide a brush, and protect glass with masking tape or use a paint shield as you work.
- Peel off tape when the paint is touch-dry. Remove any dry paint from the glass carefully with a scalpel or razor blade.

left Doors and windows should be painted in the order shown here.

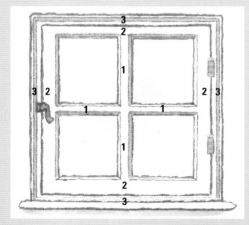

tips of the trade

- The job will be quicker if you remove all furniture and cover the floor completely with polythene sheeting.
- Take doors (especially panelled ones) off their hinges and paint them flat, supported on trestles. When you re-hang the doors, fit rising butts to make them easier to take off next time.
- Paint in a well-ventilated area, and in good light (ideally daylight).
- Keep children and pets out of the way, and store paint and tools away from curious little fingers.
- Never use a brush with a rusty ferrule as this will discolour the paint.
- If paint is a little 'blobby', strain it through an old stocking into a clean can.
- Turn cans upside down briefly and spin for a few seconds before storing. This will prevent a skin forming.
- Store paint in a cool, dry place free from frost.
- Paint the lid of the tin, so you can see the colour at a glance when you need to do a little touching up.

'Don't waste time painting poor surfaces – thorough preparation is the secret to successful decorating'

choosing wallcoverings

Walls can be decorated in many different ways, but one of the simplest and quickest ways to bring about

a change of scene is to hang a wallcovering – there is a wide choice available.

standard wallpaper available in a wide range of patterns and prices, including expensive hand-blocked and hand-printed papers that demand specialist handling. Standard papers are not washable or stain-resistant.

washable wallcoverings have a transparent plastic protective finish that makes them stain-resistant. They can be wiped or lightly sponged, but not saturated.

lining paper plain, inexpensive paper used before painting or under an expensive wallcovering. It is hung vertically before painting or horizontally before papering.

ready-pasted wallpaper a dried crystalline paste on the back is activated when immersed in water. It is easy to hang because there is no need for paste or brushes, but you may still need to paste down any seams that start to lift.

vinyls tough and scrubbable. Vinyls must be hung with a paste containing a fungicide, and it is important to ensure that the seams do not overlap.

There are three main types of vinyl wallcovering. Heavy-duty 'contoured' vinyl is sometimes called tiling-on-a-roll. Blown vinyl, where the pattern stands out in relief can be bought uncoloured, for over-painting. Blown vinyl is washable, but the surface scuffs easily. Foamed polyethylene is lightweight, slightly spongy and warm to the touch. It is hung by pasting the wall, which makes it easy to work with, although it scuffs easily.

foil metallized plastic film fused to a paper backing and overprinted with a pattern. Foil can be difficult to hang, and care must be taken around electrical fittings. The shiny surface shows up any imperfections beneath.

relief or embossed papers heavy-duty papers with a raised surface. Good for covering up poor plaster. They are designed for overpainting, usually with emulsion or eggshell, but are tough enough to take an oil-based gloss paint.

There are three main types of relief or embossed wallpaper. Woodchip contains chips of wood to create a texture like oatmeal or porridge, with

far left Borders add extra interest on a wall and can be used to outline a feature, to create panels or as a frieze. **centre** Choose a patterned wallpaper to help create a specific style. This design suggests Victorian Gothic and echoes the form of the metal bed frame. **left** Subtle contrasts in pattern and colour will help to hide ugly features and enhance good ones.

different grades from fine to coarse. It is a cheap type of wallcovering and is ideal for covering less than perfect surfaces.

Anaglypta is a trade name. This paper can look like finely modelled plaster, and some patterns relate to specific period styles. It is made from wood pulp or cotton fibres, or a vinyl version is available.

Lincrusta is made from linseed oil and fillers and formed into panels rather than bought on a roll. It is often modelled to resemble panelling and used on the lower part of the wall, then painted or stained to resemble wood. This paper is difficult to hang.

Flock is a different type of embossed paper, with a velvety pile. It is expensive, and difficult to hang and to clean, although a washable vinyl version is easier to handle.

right Here the embossed wallpaper creates a subtle contrast to the smooth textures of the furniture and accessories.

when you buy

Make sure all the rolls you buy have the same batch number. Choose the right paste for the paper (check the advice on the roll label), and make sure you have enough. A paper with a pattern repeat will need to be matched at every join. Sample books and the wrapping label will give the repeat measurement, and the larger the pattern the greater amount of wastage you will need to allow for. For a large, bold pattern you may also need to allow for a dominant element to 'sit' well on the wall – awkward breaks such as headless animals are less noticeable at the bottom of the wall than at the top.

how to hang wallpaper

Hanging wallpaper is not difficult, but it is essential that you apply it to a properly prepared surface,

otherwise imperfections in the wall will be obvious and your efforts will be wasted.

before you start

Walls should be smooth, clean, dry (see page 43) and if necessary sealed with diluted paste containing a fungicide. All woodwork should be painted and dry. Place the pasting table under a window facing the light, so you will be able to see where you have pasted.

tools

- ladders and scaffold board or scaffold platform
- pasting table
- suitable adhesive, large bucket and stirrer, or water trough for ready-pasted papers
- pasting brush
- rule and measuring tape
- plumb line and chalk or pencil
- long-bladed scissors
- paper-hanging (smoothing) brush
- sponge
- seam roller (not for embossed papers)

order of work

Start at the main window, working away from the light towards the longest unbroken wall. When you reach the corner, go back and work from the other side of the window. If the room has a chimney breast or other focal point, centre a length of paper on it and work outwards to left and right, lapping around the edge of the chimney breast.

left This simple striped wallcovering adds height to a low-ceilinged room, and provides a neutral background to the soft furnishings.

cutting and hanging

1 Measure the 'drop' and cut the first piece of paper to length, adding about 12 cm (5 in) to allow for trimming.

2 Cut several more lengths, matching up the pattern exactly to the neighbouring piece each time. Number them in sequence to avoid mistakes.

3 Take a window as your starting point, not a corner. From the edge of the frame, measure the width of the paper, less 12 mm (½ in) and mark on the wall. Suspend the plumb line from ceiling height to coincide with your mark. Draw the vertical in pencil or chalk.

4 Lay the first length of paper face down on the pasting table, slightly overlapping the edge to avoid getting paste on the table. Weigh it down so it does not roll up. Paste evenly and liberally right to the edges. If the paper is longer than the table, let the pasted paper overhang while you paste the rest. Fold ends to middle, pasted sides facing, and leave to absorb the paste.

5 To hang, hold the top corners and start to unfold and press the top of the paper to the wall, sliding it to line up with your vertical guideline. Smooth downwards and outwards with the paper-hanging brush. Open the bottom fold and continue smoothing the paper down the wall.

6 Run the back of your scissors along the angle of the ceiling and wall then peel back the paper and cut along the crease. Smooth the paper back into place. Do the same at the bottom and check for air bubbles.

7 Paste the next length and hang edge to edge (butt joined) with the previous piece – do not overlap. Except on embossed paper, gently run a seam roller down the seam.

8 Continue hanging lengths, in the order described. You will need to cut slightly shorter lengths above a radiator. Leave about 15–20 cm (6–8 in) for tucking and smoothing down behind the radiator. Sometimes it is advised to remove the radiator before papering, but this can cause problems with the heating system.

note

Ready-pasted paper is dealt with in the same way but, instead of pasting, soak each rolled length in the water trough according to instructions. Pull it out top edge first.

papering tricky areas

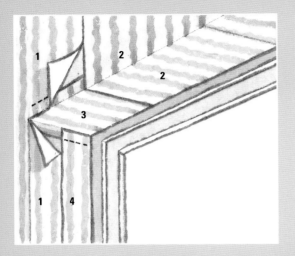 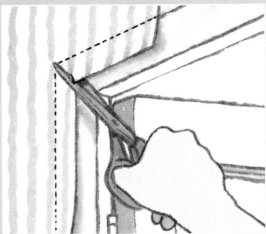 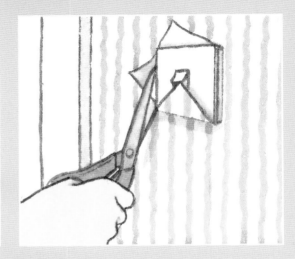

window recesses

Follow the numbered sequence in the diagram, allowing for small overlaps where indicated by the dotted line. Cut a special piece of paper for area 3 with small overlaps to tuck behind 1 and 4.

around a door

Hang a full drop of paper as though the door were not there, then cut away the surplus to within 2–3 cm (1 in) of the frame. Make a diagonal cut at the top edge, as shown, and crease the overlap top and side into the frame with the back of the scissors. Peel back, trim and smooth back into place.

switches and sockets

Switch off the power supply. Paste paper down over the fitting, then cut a cross in the paper, taking care not to scratch the switch plate. Trim back paper leaving about 1 cm (½ in). Loosen plate screws, tuck in paper and re-tighten. Do not tuck metallic or foil wallcoverings behind switch plates, just trim round the edge.

'When papering, clear up trimmed, pasted offcuts as you go'

50

tips of the trade

- When stripping old paper, score it and soak with water containing liquid detergent. Scrape it off from the bottom of the wall upwards, taking care not to dig into the plaster. If using a steam stripper always wear strong waterproof gloves and safety goggles.

- If you have never hung wallpaper before and think you will find pattern-matching difficult, choose a random pattern for your first attempt.

- Use heavy-duty fungicidal paste for vinyls and conventional paste for other papers, mixed to the right consistency for the weight of the paper. Some papers carry instructions to paste the wall, not the paper.

- Allow time for the paper to absorb the paste before hanging, and give the same 'soaking' time to every length. Heavy-duty papers need longer.

- A seam roller will flatten embossed papers and make the joins obvious, but is useful when adding a border. Dampen the area to be covered by the border and press with the seam roller to provide a flat surface.

- Heavyweight embossed papers are not a good choice on ceilings; they may be too heavy to stick firmly and could come down on unsuspecting heads.

- A random pattern will help flatten out any angles you want to disguise.

- Bold geometric patterns can look as though they are sliding off any wall that is not perfectly straight.

- Tie a plastic bag or bin liner to the ladder for sticky offcuts; leave them on the floor and you'll find yourself treading sticky footprints into other rooms.

- If you have to make a horizontal join, do not use a straight cut – tear the paper across slightly unevenly and overlap for an almost invisible join.

- Paper often bubbles when first hung but dries flat. Prick any remaining air bubbles with a pin and smooth out.

- To remedy any curling seams, ease open the seam, dab on a little paste with a cotton bud and smooth back with a seam roller.

- Make sure you hang patterned paper the right way up!

- When hanging grasscloth, brush each length in place with vertical downward strokes only, to avoid loosening any of the strands.

left Use simple textured wallcoverings to disguise a poorly plastered surface or to add subtle pattern interest.

choosing tiles

Tiling is perfectly feasible for the average home handy person, but it is a good idea to start with a small project, such as a basin splashback. Avoid anywhere that requires any tricky tile cutting, and choose tiles that don't need any complicated pattern-matching.

ceramic tiles

Most wall tiles are made from a thin slab of clay decorated with a coloured glaze, and often with a pattern. There are many shapes beyond the usual squares and rectangles, including hexagonal, octagonal, curved Provençal styles and small 'drop-ins'.

The most common square tiles are either 10 cm (4 in) or 15 cm (6 in). Rectangular tiles are usually 20 x 10 cm (8 x 4 in) and 20 x 15 cm (8 x 6 in). Border tiles, used to finish off the top edge of a panel, usually relate in size to the standard square and rectangular tiles, but are narrower in depth.

'Universal' tiles have several glazed edges, useful where you would otherwise be left with an unglazed edge exposed.

You can also buy feature panels – sets of tiles that form a large design. These can be used alone, rather like a piece of artwork, or set into a wall of plainer tiles.

left A simple geometric pattern created with plain and patterned tiles makes an attractive splashback above a basin.

other types of tiles

mosaic are tiny tiles supplied made-up on a mesh backing, usually 30 cm (12 in) square. They may be different tones of plain colours or form a distinct pattern. The sheets are laid in a bed of adhesive and then grouted. Faux mosaics are standard tiles scored to look like mosaic.

cork tiles are usually fixed as panels, rather than covering a whole wall, although cork has good insulating properties. Ideal for pin boards or feature walls. Most come in 'natural' colours, although some may be stained or dyed. Unsealed tiles are thick and crumbly, so it is better to choose the pre-sealed type. Cork can be sealed after hanging, but as it is very porous it may need many coats.

metallic and mirror tiles are often used for their reflective value. The metallic tiles are usually produced in a lightweight metal such as aluminium, made to simulate copper, pewter or stainless steel and some have interesting textures and self-patterns. They are fixed by self-adhesive pads. Mirror tiles are much heavier, and come in a wide range of sizes. Some are hung using a special adhesive, but heavier panels need to be fixed by means of special plates or mirror screws. Choose very high-quality tiles for a bathroom, as condensation can cause the silvering on the back of cheap mirror to perish.

Reflective tiles must be hung on an especially flat surface, or you will get a distorted reflection. If necessary, fix them to a panel of chipboard or hardboard and then attach this to the wall.

right Textured tiles look less clinical than the more conventional flat, glazed tiles, and add an extra visual dimension to this kitchen wall.

designing with tiles

A vast area of plain tiles in the same colour can appear cold and boring, and simply breaking up the space with a few 'drop-ins' in a vague abstract pattern always looks very static. Instead try to be bold and create an original look.

patterning with plain tiles

You can achieve amazing results using just plain square tiles:

- Hang them diagonally for a more interesting, diamond-quilted look.
- Create bold stripes with two or more colours; these could run either horizontally or vertically.
- Cut in half diagonally, a square tile becomes a triangle. Use these to form a zig-zag border, perhaps in two alternating colours.
- Create a patchwork effect with tiles of the same size and thickness but using different colours.

visualizing

It is often difficult to judge how tiles will look when covering a large expanse. Some retailers have comprehensive catalogues showing room sets, others have samples mounted on display boards. Avoid eye-boggling effects or trendy colours of which you might tire easily and take care how you use strong geometric effects: these will only work where all walls and corners are straight and true.

right The plain, neutral tiles used here give this bathroom a clean, fresh look.

pattern planning

Plan a complex design by first drawing the area on a squared grid – if you are using square tiles, one square can equal one tile.

Plot the pattern on the grid and colour in to suggest the finished design. This will enable you to see the effect and help you to work out accurate quantities.

Centre your design on any feature it relates to, such as a window or sink, and use your plan to foresee and avoid awkward cuts. Whether you choose the middle of a tile or the meeting of two tiles as the mid-point (design permitting) may make a big difference to the amount of cutting you have to do.

Whether or not you have planned the design on paper, lay out your tiles in a 'dry run' on the floor or a table. Make a rough sketch that shows where the tiles go, and if necessary number the tiles so you fix them in the right sequence.

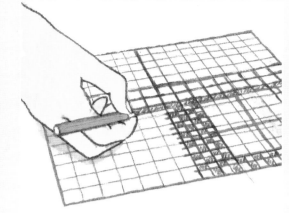

left Patterned tiles need to be carefully hung or laid to avoid awkward breaks, or mismatched designs, so work out your layout on paper first, using a grid to help you get it right.

where to use tiles

In addition to the conventional places – the 'wet' areas of the bathroom and kitchen – think about tiles for:

- The dining room, as an integral part of a food-serving surface.
- The lower part of a hall wall, to create a hard-wearing area impervious to knocks.
- Recesses or alcoves – perhaps mirror tiles as a background to glass shelving.
- A dark area, where mirror tiles might suggest a window.
- The bedroom, for example you could tile the back of the door or wardrobe doors with mirror or metallic tiles.
- Tops of tables and other items of furniture. This can be a good way of giving a new lease of life to an old item or a junk shop find.
- Kitchen worktops. You can buy special tiles for worktops, although you can also use ordinary tiles. Don't choose very highly glazed tiles, since you don't want hot pans sliding about. Sudden heat can also shatter ordinary tiles.

right When a tiled floor meets at the base of a tiled wall, try to line up any pattern or grouting. Here the grouting lines up, even though the floor and wall tiles are of a different size.

buying tiles

Tiles are usually sold in packs or boxes, but the number in a pack can vary enormously and buying in multiples of 50 could be wasteful if you are only tiling a small area. Most retailers will split packs for you, but first you need to know how many tiles you want.

estimating quantities

If you have not planned your tile design using a scale drawing, you will need to calculate the area to be covered. For an unbroken expanse, simply multiply the height (A) by the width (B). To allow for doors, windows, radiators and so on, multiply the height (A) and width (B) of each feature, add the totals and subtract from the total wall area. This will give you the area to be tiled. To work out the number of tiles, divide the area to be tiled by the area of each tile. Always add a few extras to allow for wastage with cutting and any breakages.

borders

Unless you are using 'universal' tiles (see page 52), border tiles are the conventional way of finishing off half-tiling. Borders can be chosen to coordinate with the main tiling or to contrast with it and there are some highly decorative deep-profile tiles available. Check that the border tiles are compatible in width with the main tiles and that the colours and glazes work together.

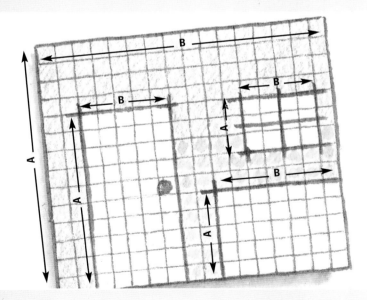

above When tiling walls you may want to sketch out the main features to scale on squared paper.

above Border tiles have been combined with plain tiles to integrate with the wall and worktop.

adhesives, grouts and sealants

Use specially formulated tile adhesive, and choose a waterproof type for wet areas. Grout, for filling the joints between tiles, is sold either as a powder or ready-mixed (which is more expensive). It comes in white and a limited range of colours, or you can colour it yourself to match your scheme. Waterproof grout is preferable, and should always be used on tiled worktops and tabletops, to provide a hygienic and impervious finish. Where tiling abuts baths, basins or shower trays you will need silicone sealant to waterproof the joint.

preparation

Tiles must be fixed to a dry, flat surface. Re-plaster any badly damaged areas and fill small holes and cracks with proprietary filler. To tile an uneven area it may be better to hang the tiles on chipboard or hardboard rather than directly on the wall. You can either fix the board to the wall with battens and then tile it, or tile the board while it is horizontal and then fix it up with impact adhesive.

Tiles can be fixed on top of previous tiling, as long as the original tiles are firmly stuck. Use a moulded tile with quite a deep profile, or a wooden trim, to hide any visible joins between the two sets of tiles.

safety note
Wear heavy-duty gloves and goggles to cut or drill tiles – the glaze can be as sharp as a shard of glass.

tile sizes

The best size of tile to use depends on the area to be covered. Larger tiles obviously work better for large expanses of wall, whereas smaller tiles work well in small rooms – such as bathrooms – where the tiles have to coordinate with fittings. Small tiles make for easier cutting and shaping around awkward areas such as built-in fixtures, recesses and window rebates. Another consideration is the effect that different sizes of tile will create in the room. Smaller tiles create a busier look, rectangular tiles are good for creating interesting herringbone and other traditional brickwork patterns, and there are other shapes that interlock for special decorative effects.

right Plain tiles can be used on their own or teamed with patterned or border tiles – the possiblities are endless.

57

how to hang tiles

Hanging tiles is not too difficult, but you need to work to a master plan – work out exactly how to position the tiles

before you start, otherwise you could end up with a tile cut in an awkward position – or a mismatched pattern.

before you start

Make sure you have all the necessary tools to cut and fix your tiles (see page 59), and ensure walls are smooth, clean and dry. (See Preparation, page 57.)

hanging tiles

1 Tiles are hung from the bottom of the wall working upwards, so first establish a perfectly horizontal base. Measure one tile depth up from the floor, skirting (baseboard) or worktop. Attach a temporary batten to the wall with long nails, using a spirit level to check it is horizontal and aligned to your measured point. Fix a vertical batten in a similar way, so its inner edge marks the edge of the last whole tile. If your design has a mid-point, mark the centre and measure out from this.

2 Apply tile adhesive to the wall with a serrated spreader. Cover only about a metre or yard at a time, and keep the container covered, as the adhesive can go off fairly quickly.

3 Press the first row of tiles firmly into place, inserting spacers between each tile. Work up the wall, and when you reach an obstacle such as a window, carry on fixing the whole tiles, leaving tile cutting until later. Keep checking that the tiles line up in both directions and that any pattern matches.

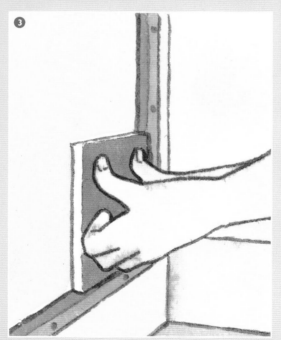

4 Once all the whole tiles are fixed, remove the battens. You are now ready to hang the cut tiles round the edges. You may have to put adhesive on the backs of these part-tiles, rather than on the wall.

5 Once the tiling is done and the adhesive is dry (allow at least 12 hours), remove the spacers. Mix the grout to a creamy paste with water and press it into the joints with a sponge or small spreader. Remove the excess with a clean, damp sponge and, for a professional finish, draw a small round-ended stick – an ice-lolly stick is ideal – to compress and finish the joints. Polish the tiles with a clean, dry cloth.

cutting tiles

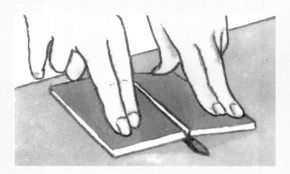

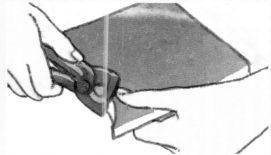

cutting straight edges
Measure where the tile is to be cut and mark on the glazed side with a felt-tip pen. Score the glazed surface firmly. Place a matchstick beneath the scored line. Press the tile down firmly either side and it should snap cleanly.

cutting curves
To cut a curved or angular shape, score the shape in the same way, then nibble away the excess with pincers or tile nibblers. You can also use a tile saw. Smooth rough edges with coarse sandpaper or carborundum stone.

tools for cutting

- felt-tip pen (use only on the glazed face)
- tile scorer
- pincers or nibblers
- tile saw
- coarse sandpaper or carborundum stone

tools for fixing

- battens
- tape measure
- spirit level
- pencil
- hammer and long masonry nails
- adhesive and notched spreader
- sponge and clean cloth
- tile spacers or matchsticks
- grout and spreader

tiling tricky areas

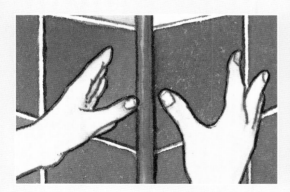

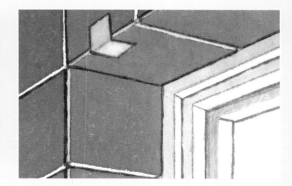

external corners
Ideally, use tiles with glazed edges, so that there is no raw edge facing out. Alternatively use a trim strip (see diagram) and ensure the tiles align on either side.

internal corners
Overlap one tile over the other in the least noticeable way and ensure any pattern matches.

window recesses
Tile the underside of the recess last and tape the tiles in position until the adhesive has fully dried.

tips of the trade

- Try to avoid having to cut pieces of tile less than a quarter of the tile width.

- If planning your tile layout on a squared grid, use a tracing-paper overlay to see where tiled edges will fall best – more convenient than having to keep marking and erasing alternatives.

- Another option is to take a photograph of the area to be tiled (beware of distorted parallels in a large area) and then use an acetate or tracing-paper overlay to help judge the best layout.

- Especially when using plain or marbled tiles, open the boxes and 'shuffle the pack' to mix the tiles before hanging. This way any colour variations in the glaze will not be immediately obvious.

- You can use floor tiles on walls, although they are likely to be heavier and more expensive, but don't use wall tiles on floors because they are not strong enough (for more on floor tiles, see pages 76–77).

- For tiled worktops use a blockboard, chipboard or plywood base. Kitchen worktops will need edging first – a wood trim is a good choice. In the bathroom, where tiles will generally run to the edge of the counter, finish with a plastic tile-edging trim.

- To drill through a tile already in position on the wall, criss-cross masking tape across the surface before you start. This will stop the drill slipping and, when you peel away the tape afterwards, the small pieces of drilled tile should come away with it.

right Be creative with magical mosaics – here they have been used to add an extra visual dimension to a bathroom wall.

CHAPTER FOUR

flooring

which type of flooring?

Floors take a lot of punishment: feet tramp across, bringing in wet, mud and grit from outside; fidgety feet scuff the same patch in front of chairs or sofas; tracks are worn where there is only one possible route across a room. There is nothing worse than spending time and effort laying a floor, to find it looks scruffy after a few months or requires tremendous upkeep.

the options

There are three basic types of flooring:

hard this includes stone, wood and ceramic tiles.

resilient such as vinyl, linoleum and rubber.

soft which includes both carpets and rugs and 'natural' coverings, such as sisal.

The different types of flooring are explored in more detail further on, but before you commit yourself to stripping old floorboards or laying a marvellous expanse of marble, consider objectively the look you want, what demands you will put on the floor and how much you can afford.

practical considerations

- How much wear and tear will the floor receive? Floors that get a lot of heavy use or through-traffic will need to be hard-wearing.
- Does it need to be washable? Halls, bathrooms, kitchens and children's rooms all need to be easy to clean and resistant to dirt and stains.
- Do you want a permanent flooring – a wise choice for kitchens, conservatories and halls – or something that will not be too difficult to change?
- Do you need a type of flooring that you can lay yourself, or is there enough in the budget to pay for it to be fitted? Large pieces of sheet material or rolls of carpet can be quite difficult to handle if you are inexperienced.

right Stylish limestone slabs look good in halls, kitchens, dining rooms or conservatories, and are easy to clean and maintain.

design considerations

- The flooring needs to relate to the style of the room or area. It is a significant proportion of the room's surface decoration, so it will not go unnoticed.

- Strong colours and bold patterns may appear to hit you in the eye, so avoid these where you want to create a relaxing mood.

- Where much of the floor is covered up with furniture or equipment, it may be a waste of effort to design a patterned floor that will not be appreciated. Interesting patterns often look best in halls, kitchens, corridors and large, sparse rooms.

- Consider the size of any pattern in relation to the scale of the room. Pale colours and small patterns can look disappointing on a large floor.

- When planning a patterned floor, whether in tiles or as a painted design on wood, think about how the pattern relates to the room's configuration. There is nothing worse than an awkward 'break' in the design at a doorway, or in front of a fireplace. Working out the design on a scale plan is always helpful.

- Collect samples and look at them in the room where you propose to use them, to gauge their effect in situ.

When you have drawn up your list of criteria, read pages 68–69 Hard Flooring, 72–73 Resilient Flooring and 78–81 Soft Flooring, to help you decide on the best solution for you.

right Wood is often the flooring of choice. Old floorboards look wonderful when restored, sanded and sealed.

preparing your floor

Whatever type of flooring you choose it will need to be laid on a sub-floor that is smooth, clean, level and dry. Problems such as damp or rot cannot be ignored and will need to be cured before you start work.

There are several ways to level an uneven sub-floor:

- Cover with flooring-grade chipboard or hardboard. Lay the latter smooth side uppermost if you will be covering with adhesive, or rough side uppermost to give a better grip for underlay and soft floorings.
- Use a floor-levelling compound. This comes as a powder that is mixed and poured over the floor, where it finds its own level and sets.
- Dig up and re-screed. These are both jobs for the professional.

Old floorboards are likely to be uneven and may have been cut to install pipes and cables. If these are to be covered with a soft or resilient flooring, the ridges will show through as wear in the new flooring, even with an underlay. Prepare old floorboards in the following way:

- Fill wide gaps with fillets of wood and narrow gaps with papier mâché.
- Repair or replace any damaged boards.
- Punch down nail heads (at least 3 mm (⅛ in) below the surface if you are going to sand).
- Screw down any loose boards (checking beneath for cables and pipes).

tips of the trade

- Always buy the best quality flooring you can afford. Price is usually a good guide – if a good carpet is beyond your budget, look at cheaper alternatives rather than very cheap carpets.
- When levelling a floor with chipboard or hardboard panels, stagger the joins so they do not align with existing boards. Remember to leave some 'trap doors' to allow for any future access.
- Old floorboards can be turned over – the underside should be smooth and the wood aged and seasoned. Call on professionals to do this as it is a major job and will involve removing and replacing skirting boards (baseboards).
- When painting, staining or tiling a floor, start in the corner furthest away from the door and work backwards towards the door opening.
- Where two different floorings meet at a doorway, you may have to install a threshold. Metal ones look very utilitarian, so use wooden ones, which are easy to stain or paint to match the floor or décor.
- To create an impression of space, use a similar flooring, or the same colour flooring throughout – particularly effective in small flats or apartments, and bungalows.
- Never lay new carpet on top of old carpet or underfelt, as the worn areas will quickly work through to the new carpet.
- Don't be tempted to pour concrete over an existing hard floor you don't like – this will damage it for ever. Calling in a salvage company will save it for someone who likes it and also boost the budget towards your new flooring.
- Try to use manufacturers' own adhesive or sealants.
- Always ask about aftercare instructions, to avoid spoiling a good floor with the wrong treatment.

'Always aim to work with what you have already got. Reclaim and restore existing floors for an authentic look'

left Old tongue-and-groove floorboards can often be restored – these have been stripped and sanded smooth and are ready for painting or staining and sealing.

hard flooring

Laying a hard floor is usually a job for the professionals, since materials are heavy to handle and require precise fitting. However, there are some types that you can fit yourself.

for

- Hard-wearing.
- Looks good and even improves with time.
- Easy to maintain and stain-resistant if sealed.

against

- Unyielding underfoot (not the best choice for the kitchen of a compulsive cook).
- Noisy, so rarely practical in a flat or apartment – many leases stipulate soft floorcovering for all floors in flats.
- Heavy. The sub-floor or joists may need strengthening, especially upstairs. May become slippery when wet.

brick is effective in halls, living areas of period homes and conservatories, but impractical for kitchens. It is crumbly and porous if not sealed.

ceramic tiles work well in halls, kitchens, dining rooms and conservatories. They are thicker and stronger than wall tiles, and without the high glaze that could make them slippery. Never lay wall tiles on floors.

quarry tiles are made of tough clay in various earthy colours. They are usually porous, so may need sealing. Good anywhere, a rustic look is preferred.

terracotta tiles can be brittle. Buy recycled tiles from a salvage company or new ones with a slightly 'distressed' surface.

encaustic tiles, also called Victorian tiles because they are often found in entrance halls and porches of this period. The pattern, usually geometric or heraldic, is constructed as an inlay that never wears.

concrete is common as a sub-floor in modern homes, but makes a hard-wearing top floor if smoothed (but not polished) and sealed with special non-slip resin. Concrete can be laid as slabs or poured on site, coloured with pigment or embedded with decorative materials.

stone original flagstones are still found in period homes, which proves their long-lasting quality. Now many types of stone make practical and attractive flooring. A cheaper option is reconstituted stone slabs, as sold by garden centres, which can be used indoors if they are adequately sealed.

slate floor tiles are usually slightly roughened (riven), making them non-slip and safe underfoot, but not so easy to clean. Ensure slate is flooring quality, not for roofs or wall cladding.

wood In many houses, though less so in newer ones, suspended floors are made from floorboards fixed to the joists. Old boards can be restored (see pages 70–71) and battered ones can be turned and relaid (a job for the expert). Flooring can also come as wood-block, laid in herringbone patterns, or intricately patterned

parquet. If you have either type, you may have to do some restoration work, but do not paint an old parquet floor.

Wood strips, panels and veneers are alternatives to solid wood. They are constructed of a thin layer (veneer) of wood on a cheaper backing. Some are suitable for laying by non-professionals. Do not confuse man-made 'wood laminate' with real wood (see pages 72–73).

plywood can be used as a floor in its own right, or for levelling a sub-floor. A birch- or maple-faced plywood can look very stylish in a modern living room.

left A change of floor level can help to separate a dual-purpose room. Here the tiles are laid to suggest greater width and the skirtings are tiled to match.

right top Victorian tiles make a stylish, yet durable floor for an entrance hall.
right Wide floorboards may need the gaps filling with fillets of wood or papier mâché.

facelifts for existing floors

If you have an existing wooden floor there is nothing to compare with the satisfaction of restoring it to its natural beauty. Sanders are not difficult to hire and make the job much easier, although you may need to finish off some areas by hand. This can be heavy and time-consuming work so pace yourself, and take adequate 'work breaks'.

before you start

Check for loose and damaged boards and remedy as necessary (see page 66). Sweep up all dust and debris. Seal the door with masking tape to keep dust from the rest of the house and open the windows so you are working in a well-ventilated space.

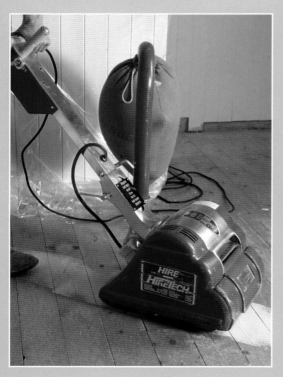

sanding a wood floor

Insist the hire shop staff show you how to use the machines and provide a full set of instructions.

Sanding is a very noisy business, so only work during sociable hours and warn your neighbours (they might like to go out for the day!).

sanders

Hire these for the day or weekend. You will need:

- A large drum machine.
- A small belt or orbital sander for the edges, or a sanding attachment on a drill.
- Coarse, medium and fine abrasive strips for each machine.
- Ear defenders, goggle and face mask.

important

Ensure the floor is solid wood since a sander will pulverize wood strip, wood mosaic panels, parquet or other veneers.

left Hiring a heavy-duty sander, such as the one shown here, will make the time-consuming job of sanding much quicker.

1 Wearing the safety equipment, begin with the big sander and a coarse abrasive sheet. Work diagonally across the floor, taking care not to knock the skirting boards (baseboards).

2 Change to a medium-grade abrasive and sand parallel with the direction of the boards.

3 Finally, switch to a fine-grade abrasive, again working in the direction of the boards. Empty the dust bag frequently, and vacuum up wood dust from the floor.

4 Use the orbital sander or the sanding attachment on your drill to deal with edges and corners. Again, work through the different grades of abrasive paper.

5 Finish by hand-sanding any areas the machines have missed.

6 Vacuum thoroughly, including windowsills and crevices between the boards. Wipe over the floor with a soft cloth soaked in white spirit, to remove any remaining dust.

painting

Create a geometric pattern or an eye-catching border, simulate a rug or give your floor a faux marble or tile effect: the possibilities are limitless.

wooden floors

1 Start in the corner furthest from the door so you have a clear exit and begin by applying a thinned coat of varnish to the whole floor. Allow to dry.

2 When marking out your design use chalk and a rule to keep lines crisp, and low-tack masking tape to delineate the edge of each colour as you work.

3 Now apply the paint, making sure your brushstrokes go in the direction of the wood's grain (length of floorboards). For any special effect, such as marbling, make sure you do a trial run on some spare wood first.

4 Remove masking tape carefully and allow each coat to dry thoroughly before protecting all paintwork with several topcoats of varnish.

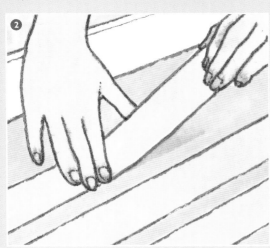

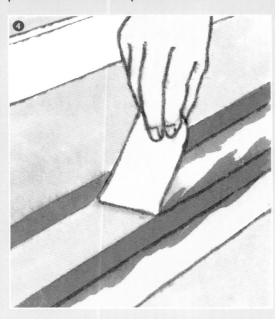

'Water-based floor paints give a more solid effect than coloured stains and give a new lease of life to unattractive boards'

staining and sealing

Oils and varnishes darken or yellow wood slightly, and woodstains can come up much stronger than on a shade card, so test first on a spare piece of sanded wood or in an unobtrusive corner. An undercoat of varnish thinned with white spirit will dilute the effect of a stain. Each finish will need several coats. Lightly sand between coats to 'key' the surface for the next coat, and wipe away dust with a cloth and white spirit.

safety note
Always use a matt or semi-matt varnish on floors.

reviving vinyl or linoleum...

Special makeover paint can bring new life to tired vinyl or lino. Try:
- a simple border effect outlining architectural features or defining kitchen units or bathroom fittings
- printing a Victorian tiled look with sponges cut into geometric shapes
- stencilling a unique patterned flooring. There is no need to varnish the floor after using this paint.

...and concrete

Industrial floor paints can transform a concrete or cement floor. A chequerboard effect can look stunning.

resilient flooring

These floorcoverings are less noisy and kinder underfoot than hard floorings, but firmer than carpet. Resilient floors are made in both natural and man-made materials. Some are available in extra-broad widths to fit a large room without seams or joins, others come as tiles that are easy to lay.

for

- Comfortable underfoot.
- Practical alternative to hard flooring where soft floorcoverings are not suitable.
- Low-maintenance.
- Often easy to lay.
- Many suit a small budget.

against

- Those masquerading as traditional flooring are usually unconvincing.
- The cheapest ranges can prove a poor buy.
- Most are unsuitable with underfloor heating.

left Resilient flooring, such as linoleum, vinyl or rubber, works well in multi-purpose rooms where ease of care and cleaning is important.

cork the bark of the cork-oak is light, warm and a natural insulator that deadens sound. It also swells when wet, so must not be exposed to damp. Colours are usually warm browns, but can be combined with a coloured underlay, which will glow through. Tiles are available either sealed or unsealed, and you should treat unsealed tiles with several coats of wax or polyurethane varnish after laying. Suitable for any room.

linoleum, or lino, is a natural product made from linseed oil, resin, wood flour and fillers, spread onto a hessian (burlap) backing and cured to create a very flexible, hard-wearing flooring. Available in exciting colours and effects, for any room in the house except the stairs. Sheet lino is best fitted professionally (especially if you want a laser-cut inlaid design), but tiles are comparatively easy to lay, and you can buy coordinating borders and strips.

rubber is back in fashion as a flooring. It is warm, very resilient and quiet, and comes in a wide range of colours. Some of the heavily studded surfaces can be difficult to clean. Contrary to expectations, it is not ideal for a bathroom or shower room as it can perish if saturated with water. Rubber comes in sheets (best laid by a professional) and DIY tiles, the latter of which can be used on stairs (see page 82).

laminates include woodgrain effects (often called wood laminate), marble and a host of individual designs. They need no sealing or polishing and can be cleaned with a damp cloth. They are suitable for most rooms except bathrooms where they could swell and start to lift if saturated.

vinyl is often used to imitate tiles, wood or other traditional floors, but ranges now appear in delicious colours, with interesting effects such as glitter, mother-of-pearl and metallic – marvellous in the right setting, such as a child's room or a contemporary loft or warehouse conversion. Most vinyl can be laid by a competent home owner (see page 76–77). Vinyl is more vulnerable to scratching, dents and burns than some resilient floorings and is unsuitable for stairs.
   Rigid vinyl is available as tiles and complementary borders but can be quite unyielding underfoot. Flexible vinyl can be 'lay flat', which moulds itself to the sub-floor and only needs sticking down round the perimeter, or cushioned, which gives extra bounce. It is available either in sheets or tiles (including self-adhesive).

other resilient flooring in natural materials include leather tiles (very expensive) and metal (expensive and noisy). There are vinyl and rubber simulations that achieve the same hi-tech look as metal.

safety note

An early type of synthetic floor was the thermoplastic or vinyl asbestos tile. It is essential to call in experts when removing these, as the asbestos content is hazardous to health.

above A geometric pattern, created with vinyl tiles, can define and separate parts of a room.

laying a laminate floor

Real wood is an expensive option, so if you don't have an existing floor that you can restore

(or don't want the bother of stripping), a popular alternative is a laminate or floating floor.

Laminates are formed by fusing an image of wood onto MDF (particleboard) or condensed chipboard and protecting it with layers of transparent laminate so it looks like a hard floor finish. Laminate boards resemble floorboards but are only about 10 mm (⅜ in) thick. They are tongued-and-grooved to fit together easily.

A laminate floor is easy to clean and non-allergenic, but as noisy underfoot as most hard floors. If you are laying over a hard floor, and especially in an upstairs apartment, the insulating membrane usually supplied with the laminate may not be enough. You will need to consider some form of extra insulation under the laminate or even insulating between the joists. Laminate can be laid over almost any other type of flooring, and if you predict problems with noise, you might consider laying it over a ready-fitted carpet, although this is not ideal.

before you start

Ensure the sub-floor is sound and flat (see page 66). You can remove the skirting boards (baseboards), although this is not essential and they can be fiddly to replace.

tools

- strong pair of scissors
- steel measuring tape
- pre-cut wooden spacers 6 mm (¼ in) thick
- set-square or straight-edge
- pencil
- craft knife
- hand tenon or crosscut saw
- hammer
- tapping block
- adhesive, in a glue gun

right A wood laminate laid throughout the ground floor provides visual continuity and creates the impression of a bigger space.

laying laminate boards

1 Cut the foam insulating membrane in lengths and cover the existing floor, fitting it neatly into the corners.

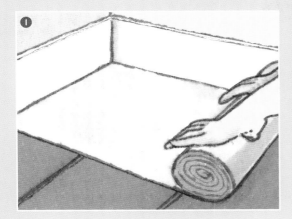

2 Start in the corner furthest away from the door. Lay the first laminate board against the wall. Spread glue sparingly on the end tongue and slot on a second board. Work down the length of the room parallel to any existing boards, inserting spacers between the boards and the wall.

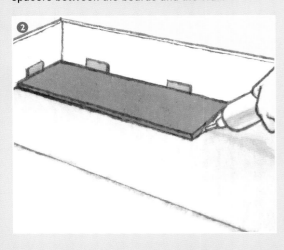

3 To complete the first row with a part-board, carefully measure and mark the board with a set-square/straight-edge and pencil. Score the mark with the craft knife and cut cleanly with the saw.

4 To lay the second row, apply the adhesive along the length as well as the end tongue. The boards will slot together quite easily. Tap them home with the tapping block and hammer. If any excess adhesive oozes out, wipe it off with a damp cloth immediately.

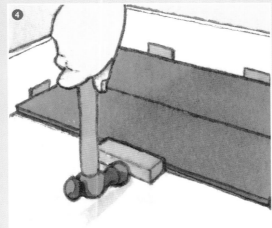

5 Continue laying the floor, length by length, across the room, staggering the joins so that you do not get a noticeable seam. You may have to cut the last row of boards lengthways to fit – remember to allow for the 6 mm (¼ in) space between the floor and the wall.

6 Leave the floor to dry, and take precautions to ensure that no one walks on it before the glue is completely set.

7 Remove all the spacers. Cut lengths of 2 cm (¾ in) quadrant (quarter-circle wood trim) to fit around the perimeter of the room, to cover the gap between the laminate and the wall. Glue the skirting (baseboard) face of the quadrant only, so the floor can still move – this is why it is called a floating floor.

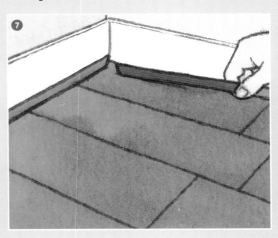

note

Although laminate flooring is tough and hard-wearing, it should not be saturated with water. Mopping the floor with excess water could cause the boards to swell and begin to push up. Use a damp mop or cloth only, and always wipe up any spills immediately.

laying floor tiles

Floor tiles, like wall tiles, can be used creatively to make whatever pattern you wish. An imaginative design can help to improve the proportions of the room – stripes laid widthways will make a floor area look less long and narrow, while a chequerboard effect will create an impression of greater space.

Just as with wall tiles, floor tiles need to be centred on the middle of the floor or dominant feature. If you are creating a pattern, draw up a scale plan of the room on gridded paper, so that you can see how best to position the pattern and how many of each colour you will need. However sure you are of your calculations, always buy a few extra tiles to allow for accidents and wastage.

Store the tiles, especially cork, linoleum and vinyl, where you are going to lay them for about 48 hours so they can acclimatize. Make sure you have the right kind of adhesive for the tile. Some vinyl tiles are self-adhesive, and simply have a peel-off backing. Unsealed cork tiles will need to be sealed after laying.

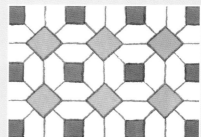

before you start

Make sure the surface that the tiles are to be laid on is stable and level. If the subfloor isn't uneven, it is best to put down hardboard or chipboard before laying the tiles.

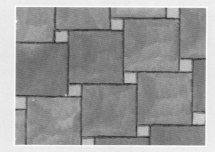
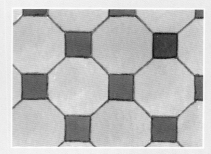

tools

- steel measuring tape
- straight-edge
- chalk line (string covered in chalk)
- pencil
- craft knife
- cutting board
- profile tool and sharp scissors, if you have to fit round specific shapes, such as bathroom fittings

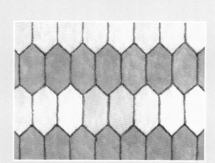

right There are lots of exciting design possibilities with resilient floor tiles – different shapes and colours will allow you to create a highly individual floor for any room in your home.

laying self-adhesive tiles

1 Find the true centre of the room by marking the centre of two opposite walls. Snap the chalk line between the two points. Do this between the other two walls and you will have the centre point of the room marked as a cross.

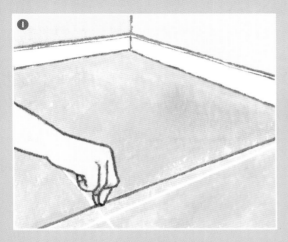

2 Lay out the tiles in a 'dry run' so that any problems come to light before you commit yourself to sticking them down.

note

These instructions are for self-adhesive vinyl tiles, which are the easiest to lay, but the principles are much the same for all tiles.

However, if the tiles are not self-adhesive, make sure you use the correct adhesive and only spread enough to fix one tile at a time.

Most of the harder types are best left to the experts: they are heavy to handle and hard to cut, and some have to be set in a bed of mortar.

3 Peel the backing off the first tile and, aligning it with two arms of the central cross, press it down lightly and firmly. Work from the centre out towards the edges, carefully butting the tiles up to each other and checking pattern matches.

4 You will probably have to cut tiles to fit around the edge. Lay a tile (do not remove the backing) over the last full tile, and mark with the pencil and straight-edge where the cut is to come.

5 Cut the tile on a board, using the craft knife against the straight-edge.

6 Peel off the backing and lay in position with the cut edge against the wall, not abutting the last full tile.

7 To cut a non-rectangular part-tile (walls are seldom perfectly straight), you will need to turn the tile over to mark the fit, or carefully measure the space. For awkward shapes, especially curves, use a profile tool to template the outline. A fiddly shape may be easier to cut with scissors.

soft flooring

The appeal of soft floorcoverings is their warmth and quiet. As well as conventional carpets and rugs, soft flooring includes 'natural' floorings made from a variety of grasses and vegetable fibres.

above Natural floorcoverings combine well with wooden floors – here a golden-beige sisal is laid as an 'inset' to contrast with restored wide wooden floorboards.

for

- Warm and cosy underfoot, although 'natural' floorcoverings less so.
- Good insulation from cold and draughts.
- Helps deaden sound.

against

- Vulnerable to staining, even if treated.
- Impractical in areas that get wet.
- Sisal and seagrass can be slippery so must not be used on stairs.

types of natural flooring

Grasses and vegetable fibres have been used for centuries as floorcoverings. Most are strong and hard-wearing, but they are, in the main, rather harsh or roughly textured, and are not really suitable for floors where children might be crawling, or where it is usual to walk around barefoot. As they can be slippery, don't use them on stairs. Some do not take colour well and tend to fade, so the undyed form is often the best choice.

Natural floorings (apart from rush matting) are laid in a similar way to carpet, although some cannot be stretched. They may need to be laid over underfelt, although some of the latex-backed varieties can be stuck to the sub-floor. When used as a close-covered carpet, all need to be professionally laid.

coir, or coconut fibre, was once only used for doormats. It is now woven into coarse but interestingly textured flooring that is sometimes dyed bright colours. It is usually supplied backed, but some narrow widths (for use in halls or corridors) are unbacked.

hemp is soft underfoot, but not as strong as some natural floorings. It is woven into attractive herringbone, ribbed and chevron textures.

jute looks similar to sisal and has a textured, ribbed weave. It is best used in areas of fairly light wear, such as bedrooms, and should be treated with a stain inhibitor.

paper twine is twisted from strong, unbleached paper and made into rugs. It can be plain, or striped in interesting colour combinations, and the slightly luminous quality adds an extra textural dimension. Paper twine is usually laid loose on top of another flooring.

rush matting is hand- or machine-plaited into strips, sewn together to form standard-size mats. 'Medieval matting' is custom-made, the strips sewn together to a specified size and bound with a small hand-woven strip. Rush matting has an interesting, heavy texture, but tends to shed fibres, creating a lot of dust.

seagrass is a tough tropical grass spun and woven into coarse matting. It is usually left undyed, in a random mix of yellow, beige, green and a hint of russet. It is hard-wearing, but not suitable for wet areas. Extra loose-laid mats are recommended as protection from furniture castors and wear in front of sofas. If laid on stairs, the grain should run parallel to the tread.

sisal is a whitish, stringy fibre, originally used for heavy-duty ropes and twine. It is woven into attractive herringbone, bouclé and ribbed patterns and comes in a range of colours; it can also be stencilled. Sisal can be used in most rooms, but is not recommended for kitchens or bathrooms. A sisal and coir blend gives a finer weave and texture that is less scratchy underfoot. Sisal can stretch (even with a backing) and may need occasional refitting (a light spray of water can help shrink it back into shape). Like rush matting, sisal is inclined to shed.

right Natural floorings come in a variety of textures from ribbed and herringbone to a simple squared effect.

carpets and rugs

Carpets are a popular option, but the choice – even before you consider colour or design – is immense. What they are made of and how they are made affects their feel and durability. Read labels carefully and take the advice of the supplier. Make sure prices quoted include the necessary underfelt and fitting.

construction methods

Woven carpet has the pile closely woven into the backing to produce a high-density surface (Axminster and Wilton refer to weaving methods, not the source of the carpet). Woven carpets are beautiful and durable, but can also be expensive. The majority of carpets in the mid-price range are non-woven. Most are tufted, made by 'needling' the pile into a backing, with a secondary backing for strength and stability.

types of carpet pile

Density of pile refers to the number of tufts per square centimetre or inch – the thicker the pile the more hard-wearing the carpet should be, and for areas of heavy use, a looped or kinked pile is a sensible choice.

close or velvet is luxurious, but will show 'tracking' where it has been walked on.

hard-twist has an extra kink in it, like curly hair. This adds to its wearability, but can make it slippery, so best not used on stairs.

long or shag is usually looped or twisted. This creates an interesting texture, but is very difficult to keep looking good.

looped has a characteristic nubbly texture. When made with mixed fibres this may 'pill' into small balls of loose fibre, so choose a 100 per cent wool (often called Berber-style).

saxony is a dense, mid-length pile, best for areas of light to medium use.

'sculptured' or 'carved' pile is a mixture of cut and looped, creating a heavily textured effect; for medium to light use.

fibres

Some fibres are more resistant to stains than others but, whatever the manufacturers claim, carpets are not truly washable, even when treated with a stain inhibitor.

wool, the traditional fibre for carpets, has a natural resilience. A mix of 80 per cent wool with 20 per cent easy-care synthetic (usually nylon) is considered to be the best fibre for carpets.

synthetics acrylic most closely resembles wood, but others include nylon in various forms, polyester, polypropylene and viscose/rayon, either on their own or combined with other fibres.

cotton is used for washable rugs and to bulk out other fibres.

silk is still used in hand-knotted oriental carpets and rugs.

underlay

Carpet will last much longer and be more comfortable if it is cushioned by an underlay. This can be the felted hairy type, or a rubber or plastic foam that increases the 'bounce' factor. Both types should be professionally fitted at the same time as the carpet.

sizing up

Narrow 'body' or 'strip' widths are used as runners for halls, and on stairs. Broadloom (woven on a wide loom) comes in multiples of 1 m (3 ft) up to 5 m (16 ft).

carpet tiles

These can be cut easily to fit round awkward shapes, making them useful for small or irregularly shaped rooms. Individual tiles can be lifted to be cleaned or replaced but, despite claims, this does not make them ideal for wet areas. They should be fixed either with a flexible adhesive at each corner or with a special double-sided tape. Carpet tiles present interesting design possibilities, such as chequerboard and chevrons, borders, stripes and checks and even, with precise cutting, inlaid motifs.

rugs

Rugs add colour and interest to a room as well as providing protection for carpet or wood – and you can take them with you when you move. Match your rugs to your style: ethnic alternatives to expensive oriental rugs include a wide variety of kelims, dhurries and animal skins, while felt, cotton and rag rugs suit a cottage style.

safety note

Lay rugs on a non-slip backing so that they do not slide on smooth floors or ruck up on carpets.

'Above all, floors should be practical and easy to clean – avoid pale colours and heavy textures in well-used areas'

left A neutral colour and heavily textured carpet looks good, and is luxurious underfoot, in an 'adults only' sitting room.

stairs

Safety is paramount when deciding on the covering for stairs: whatever you choose must be non-slip and non-trip, as well as hard-wearing.

types of stair covering

close-carpeting on the stairs is definitely a job for the expert. Not all carpets are suitable so take advice from a professional.

carpet runners leave some of the stair on either side uncovered and are much simpler to fit than close carpeting because it is held in position with stair rods, which slot into clips or eyes screwed to the base of each stair riser. The carpet can be moved up or down the stairs occasionally to even out the wear – tuck under the excess at either top or bottom of the stairs when laying. Leave the exposed wood at the sides natural or think about a colour to tone or contrast with the carpet, or a decorative paint finish such as marbling.

rubber tiles can look very effective on stairs, with some design input. Choose, for example, two contrasting colours for the tread and the riser, or have nosings (the front edge of the tread) in a different colour. Alternatively, you could create a patchwork effect with several different colours.

ceramic tiles are very suited to a Mediterranean or North African style. They are noisy, but could inspire an interesting design feature. They need to be professionally laid.

other options stairs do not have to be covered. Leave them exposed as natural wood, or paint them. You could simulate a runner and carry the design down into the hall, and paint the floor to match.

right A stair runner is fixed with traditional stair rods. It is important that the carpet is securely attached over special underfelt pads to ensure it is safe.

CHAPTER FIVE

transformations

planning a makeover

Before you rush out for tools and materials, plan carefully. Take your time – and don't indulge

in any impulse or spur-of-the-moment buys!

how far do you go?

Do you want a quick fix, or a more permanent change? Are you likely to stay in your home for some time, or will you be moving on soon? A complete transformation will need careful planning and may involve a lot of effort and mess. Often, a comparatively small change – fresh paint; a new rug or bedlinen; designing a new window treatment – can make a disproportionate difference.

what can you afford?

What you can and can't do will, to some extent, relate to your budget. You may decide to put some plans on hold while you save up for a special piece of furniture or can pay for some professional help.

what are the priorities?

Try to decide which rooms are really in need of a makeover and which can wait. The hall may beg to be done first, as it is the first area you see when you come in. The sitting room is frequently the most used area, and the previous owner's flowery wallpaper or the developer's bland magnolia paint may irritate you every time you sit down. Bedrooms are personal spaces where you can impose your personality, but are often shared, so a new look may be a joint decision. Kitchens and bathrooms are the 'working' areas and may take longer to plan.

right Using all you have learnt, from colour and style, to wallcoverings and floorings, you can now create your perfect room!

Once you have decided which area to tackle first, follow these guidelines:

assess the situation how you use the room; how to make best use of the space; and how much to spend.

plan a practical layout make a scale plan and work out where to position furniture and appliances. Don't forget to leave space for 'traffic flow'.

think about the look will your preferred style work? Frills and flounces can look good in a bedroom, but are impractical in a kitchen, and a stark modern look is not always a comfortable choice for a sitting room.

be objective what are the room's good features, and what would be better removed or camouflaged?

create a focal point fireplaces are no longer to be found in every sitting room, but installing one will create a 'heart of the home' feel. An alternative might be the view, or the window itself. Use an eye-catching piece of art or furniture, or an unusual treatment on one wall to grab attention.

think about lighting consider the three basic ways of lighting a room: background glow from ambient lighting fitted with dimmers; decorative lighting and fittings to relate to the overall style; and display lighting to spotlight a specific item or architectural feature. The cheapest, most instant form of lighting is kinetic – candles, oil lamps or flickering firelight.

don't underestimate accessories finishing touches to underline the basic style add contrast and life to your scheme. Accessories also add a personal touch.

compile a sample board (see page 36). This will ensure that you will be happy with the finished result.

draw up a schedule if you plan to redecorate the whole house, start at the top and work down, and from the back to the front.

Once you are clear about what you want to achieve and how to do it, you are ready to begin that total transformation!

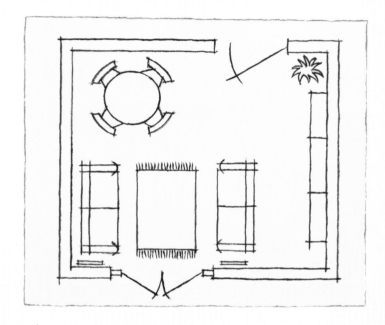

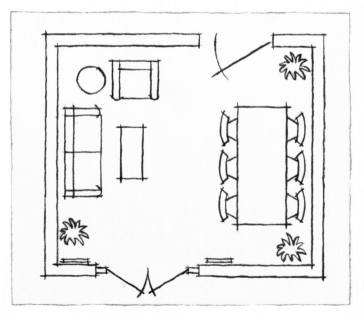

right Making several sketched plans of the room you want to redecorate can help you think about space and the best position for furniture.

the hall
from this...

This is typical of the narrow, dark hall found in many houses. It looks tired and is in need of an update.

- The floor has been stained a dark brown to hide the fact the boards are in a poor state of repair.
- The small fringed rug presents a safety hazard.
- The walls and skirting boards (baseboards) are painted a safe neutral and the front door has had the panelling picked out to contrast, which looks fussy.
- The whole area lacks any form of personality or impact.

initial thoughts
A simple change of colour scheme would instantly create a more modern look and some remedial work to the floor and the introduction of a few good accessories would transform this area.

walls can be painted and more can be made of the room's architectural features by outlining them in white.

floor can be stripped, sanded and painted.

furniture can be updated.

light and space a hall can be made to appear larger and airier with the use of cleverly positioned mirrors. These will also help it seem less narrow and not so long.

...to this

The new look is stylish, streamlined and modern. It feels welcoming and will have a positive impact on visitors.

how it was done

floor the floorboards were stripped and sanded, then painted with a special, quick-drying floor paint. The grid pattern was carefully worked out beforehand on paper.

walls easily freshened with a coat of emulsion in a light sandstone shade that tones with the floor base colour.

door repainted with crisp white gloss paint.

skirting boards (baseboards) painted to match the walls, with the beading at the top and the door frames picked out in white, to make them stand out against the walls.

finishing touches modern metal accessories – a stylish chrome and plywood chair, a metal planter and metal-framed mirrors – add reflected light to the area. The thick coir doormat is practical.

other ideas

In a period home, disguise an over-tall hall by adding a dado rail about 1 m (3 ft) from the floor and treat the areas above and below it differently – you might like to try a marbling or dragged paint effect.

Try to do something interesting with the far end of a long hall. You could paint it a strong colour, paper it with a bold pattern or clad it with mirror or metallic tiles. If there is a door in this wall, paint it to contrast with the wall.

the sitting room
from this...

The sitting room should be somewhere that you feel at ease, a room in which to talk, read or watch television. Often it is the most important room in the house and is used for many different purposes.

This sitting room has an unstructured, impermanent feel about it that does not encourage you to settle down.

- The fireplace has no character.
- A nondescript grey carpet and neutral colour scheme give the room a slightly grubby look.
- There is nowhere cosy to sit.
- The sash window (not shown) is attractive, but the view is not.
- The sill-length curtains (not shown) are limp and skimpy.

initial thoughts
A fresh colour scheme with some interesting accents, a different floor treatment, some work on the fireplace to make it a focal point and the addition of some comfortable sofas and chairs, would make this an elegant room in which to relax.

fireplace will benefit from a complete makeover.

floor can be re-covered or taken back to bare boards.

new furniture is needed, but need not be expensive.

window treatment needs to let in light but cut out draughts, and hide the view.

walls can be freshened up with a coat of paint.

accessories should be original and personal to add character.

...to this

The room now looks fresh and uncluttered. It has plenty of personal touches and a colour scheme that is at once bright but easy on the eye – an inviting space to spend time in.

how it was done

floor stripped and sanded boards were painted a creamy white, and outlined with a fine-lined red border – this emphasizes the hearth and helps make the fireplace stand out.

fireplace given a clean-cut look, with the tiles painted with a special tile paint in pale blue and cream. It is now a major focal point for the room, especially when surmounted by a bold piece of abstract art.

window floor-to-ceiling louvred shutters transform the window area. Their cool blue is picked up from the fireplace tiling and matches the tables.

furniture a classic sofa and chair provide comfortable seating to curl up in. Choosing plain cream covers has allowed for a jewel-bright collection of scatter cushions.

walls a warm cream is just the right neutral as a background for the bright accessories.

occasional tables bought cheaply and given a new lease of life with the same paint used on the shutters. The low-slung coffee table was tiled to match the fireplace and to make it very practical.

plants and accessories have been chosen for their sculptural qualities.

detailing

The bright red adds zing to a scheme that might otherwise be in danger of being a little cold. It would be easy to change to another accent colour, such as sunny yellow or rich green, to match changing moods and seasons. The choice of items to give these brilliant finishing touches also adds interest – glossy, fun little knick-knacks that can easily be swapped around or exchanged.

or try this...

A richly coloured painted border around the floor gives the effect of an ethnic rug. The rest of the room has been kept very plain so that this is a feature that doesn't get lost.

fireplace removing the fireplace surround and tiles and having the exposed area replastered created a minimalist, hole-in-the-wall display area for plants and accessories.

floor stripped and sanded and painted with a neutral colour floor paint. The bold border design was planned out to scale on paper first, then the pattern transferred to the floor, using pencil guidelines and a ruler and set-square to ensure the angles were accurate. Each colour was created separately, with the surrounding area masked off with low-tack masking tape until the paint was touch-dry. A more free-form design would have called for artistic ability, but geometric patterns, even complex ones, just need patience and accuracy.

chairs and sofa kept neutral, with a mix of bright cushions. Some are plain and others were chosen for their woven ethnic covers in colours and designs that echo the floor border.

window given a simple treatment – a roller blind (not shown) that tones with the walls and has a broad border stencilled along the bottom to match the floor border. This was done using fabric paints.

walls painted a very pale blue-grey. The radiator was painted to match, so that it merges unnoticed into the background.

the kitchen
from this...

This basic kitchen is typical of one which can be found in many properties built or refurbished in the late 1970s and early 1980s: it lacks character and style, and is short on storage.

- The colour-washed paint finish on the walls now looks tired and out of date.
- The wood-veneered units are robust but heavy-looking.
- The woodblock floor is in a good state of repair.
- The basic stainless steel sink has individual taps; common 30 years ago, but hardly used today.
- The tiled splashback behind the sink has a few patterned tiles inset to create pattern interest, but they are boring and old fashioned.
- The refrigerator, although adequate, looks dated.
- The furniture is an odd mix of hand-me-downs.

initial thoughts

It need not cost a lot of money to give this kitchen a facelift, and it isn't necessary to do any complicated replanning and refitting.

walls can be painted.

tiles and worktops can be replaced (or existing tiles painted over, using a special tile paint).

wooden floor can be stripped, sanded and either stained and sealed or painted.

sink can be updated with a simple change of taps to give a more modern look.

accent colours these can be added by using patterned or plain accessories.

...to this

This style aims towards a warm, cosy, heart-of-the-home feel, where the colours suggest spring sunshine all year round. The basics have been left in place, but recoloured to create a modern farmhouse look.

how it was done

units have been painted in a pale creamy yellow, and the old metal handles exchanged for round wooden knobs.

sink the pedestal taps have been replaced with a streamlined mixer unit. The sink has been given a thorough clean, and a new, colourful plug.

tiles have been replaced by creamy-yellow ones, with occasional mint green and lilac tiles inset to provide cool accents (this effect could also be created by painting the existing tiles).

walls have been repainted in ivory, which helps to enhance the warmer colours introduced into the scheme in the units, accessories and furniture.

floor has been stripped, and sanded back to a light wood colour then given several coats of sealant to make it practical, easy to clean and able to withstand kitchen spills.

refrigerator has been given a fashionable 'large American fridge' look, by respraying it in metallic paint.

furniture has also been given a makeover. A primrose laminated top has been added to the table and the frame has been given a light wood stain. The chairs have been painted to match the tabletop.

detailing

The country look can be softened even further by the introduction of flowers and floral patterns. They add character and enhance the farmhouse style. Here pretty floral accessories, such as cushions and napkins, to match the curtains, have been used. Some old-fashioned items can still look good in today's kitchens, while others, such as the sink's original taps, just look like leftovers from another age.

or try this...

This modern city kitchen has a more contemporary feel and would suit a loft-style apartment or modern river- or canal-side flat. A cool colour scheme can often be introduced to suggest space and light.

walls have been painted soft white. Bright white would have looked slightly clinical, and just a little too hard against the tiles.

units have also been painted white, with the plinth outlined in silver grey, to echo the new grey laminated worktop. Notice how much difference the handles make. By adding these sleek chrome handles our eyes notice the inset pattern of the doors less, and the overall effect is much plainer.

floor has been painted in creamy white with a painted mint green border to outline the units. It was then sealed with a gloss varnish to protect the paint. You could use a matt or even 'dead flat' varnish if you prefer a more muted effect.

sink the taps have been changed for a matching chrome mixer unit. There's no need to buy a very expensive unit: look for one that reflects the shape and colours you're working with, and keep it simple.

tiles the splashback has been painted a cool blue-green and re-grouted in white using a special grouting pen (these are available from DIY stores in a variety of colours).

refrigerator has been sprayed with metallic silver paint to echo the chrome (not shown).

furniture the chairs have been replaced with a set of folding metal and wood garden chairs, which were very inexpensive and can be easily folded away to create space. A simple rectangular table was painted to pull in both main colours: mint green and off-white. The two-colour effect looks fresh and clean and links in well with the rest of the colour scheme, creating a spacious feel.

the bedroom
from this...

Even if they have to be dual- or multi-purpose, bedrooms should be soothing, private places that express your own personality. This drab, dark room, with its utilitarian furniture, fails on all counts.

- Whatever a bedroom's other shortcomings, the bed should be comfortable. This is sagging and overdue for replacement.
- The dark walls make the room seem cave-like and devoid of comfort.
- There is insufficient storage for the many different items that need to be tidied away in a typical bedroom – sports and hobby equipment as well as shoes and clothes.
- Old or secondhand furniture can have great appeal, but these pieces are characterless.
- The woodwork's virtues are hidden beneath layers of peeling paint.
- The battered floorboards and thin grey carpet give the room the air of temporary student accommodation.

initial thoughts

What this room needs is some romance and personality: a relaxing colour scheme, a new bed and some practical storage, a facelift for the chest-of-drawers and some little touches of luxury.

walls need lightening and brightening.

radiator a classic that could be treated to become a feature.

furniture needs revamping or replacing, especially the bed.

accessories should be soft, colourful and personal.

floor would take a sophisticated paint treatment well.

window (not shown) a good feature but needs to be made less stark.

...to this

Stylish, romantic, feminine – this is now a bedroom you would be glad to wake up in. The toning colours are soft without being cloying, and fresh flowers, diffused light and embroidered silks contribute to the overall appeal.

how it was done

floor once stripped and sanded, the floor was given two coats of floor paint. The pale green border has emphasized the shape and architectural style of the room. A bedside rug would give extra comfort in winter.

window existing shutters at the full-length sash window were restored so they close at night, and a voile curtain filters the light and gives privacy during the day.

storage versatile mix of hanging space, drawers and shelving was built along one wall, and the doors painted to match the rest of the furniture.

chest-of-drawers checked for woodworm and the drawer runners repaired so they ran smoothly. The chest was then painted pale blue and the handles replaced.

bed the mattress was replaced and the metal frame was bought in a secondhand shop, sanded down, primed and given several coats of metallic paint. Bed knobs coordinate with the chest handles.

fabrics bedlinen and a quilted cover in pinks, lilacs and mauves complete the colour scheme, and are echoed in cushions and floral accessories.

radiators

The radiator is a classic example of an early cast-iron pillar style. It was decided to enhance its features by painting it with metallic paint, to tie in with the metal bed frame. If the radiator had not had so much character it could either have been faded into the background by painting it with the same emulsion as the walls (then protected with transparent radiator paint) or enclosed with a radiator cover.

the bathroom
from this...

The bathroom is now the most popular room for an update, but any replanning has to be carefully thought through due to the constraints of plumbing. This bathroom's fittings are still in good condition, but the decoration is looking worn and dull. Overall, the room has a slightly grimy feel even though it is kept clean — not somewhere you feel like lingering.

- The marble-effect stick-down coating on the basin-unit's doors is from a previous makeover, and now looks dated.
- The tan and beige colour scheme looks very tired.
- The floor has been stained and covered with a treacly varnish to waterproof it, but it gives an ugly finish.
- There is nothing wrong with the tiling except the colour and some ingrained dirt in the grouting.
- Accessories are uncoordinated and lacking in style.

initial thoughts

As bathrooms are often small, pale colours are usually chosen, but more strident colour schemes often work surprisingly well.

basin unit can be transformed with paint and new handles.

colour scheme should be fresh and clean-looking.

floor will need a complete facelift.

tiles can be painted to bring about a totally different look.

accessories could follow a single theme, which would add interest and fun.

sanitaryware does not have to be replaced.

...to this

The colours of sea and sky, with a seashore theme running through the accessories, give this bathroom modern appeal. Mostly the effect was achieved with imagination and an eye for colour rather than a great deal of expense, although renovating the floor was hard work.

how it was done

floor the treacly stain was scraped off and the boards were sanded smooth and painted. The pale, bleached look provided the basis for the seashore theme.

heating even the stylish new heated towel rail has a slightly nautical air, and will keep the bathroom warm as well as dry the towels.

walls freshened up with a clear, pale blue emulsion, to contrast with the white woodwork and bathroom fittings.

towels more than just a colourful accessory, velvety, enveloping towels are one of the pleasures of bathing. Extra-large ones were chosen in shades of deep jade, blue and lilac-blue.

tiles

Instead of replacing the old mottled tiles or tiling over them (awkward in the shower area), they were transformed with paint. The edge of each alternate tile was masked with low-tack masking tape, then every other tile was painted with special tile paint. The tape was removed when the paint was touch-dry, and when the paint was completely dry the exercise was repeated with the second colour. The grouting between the tiles was freshened up with a white grouting pen, which also helps to emphasize the chequerboard effect.

basin unit the old plastic was stripped off, the whole unit sanded smooth and then given a new look with soft blue paint. Neat, modern wooden handles match the under-framing and legs and were sealed to protect the wood from wet hands.

finishing touches seashells, driftwood and the unusual twiggy mirror frame suggest beachcombing finds, while plants and a small collection of coral hint at the tropics.

or try this...

A modern take on traditional themes. This bathroom has echoes of many different eras and sources, but the disparate elements, far from jarring, are brought together by colour and a unity of styling to create a room that feels pleasingly unlike a bathroom.

colour scheme limiting the colour range is key to the success of this room. Soft pink, lavender and white make a beautiful combination that, in this case, it would be a mistake to 'enhance' with a contrasting accent colour.

floor keeping the same lavender colour on the floor accentuates the cocooning effect of the room. Floor paint would have provided an opaque covering, but using emulsion has allowed a little of the wood grain to show through, like a coloured woodstain. The floor has been protected with several coats of non-slip matt varnish.

tiles to play down the 'typical bathroom' look, tiling has been kept to a minimum: a splashback for the basin and inside the shower area. The paints for walls and woodwork were mixed to match the tiles using computer colour-matching – a service offered by many paint and DIY stores.

furniture the bentwood chair and the butler's folding table with drawers (not shown) are both practical and pretty. They were chosen for their lightness – although very different in style they each have a see-through quality, which means they can be put to useful purpose without being imposing or intrusive.

detailing the filigree mirror frame and the wire and glass chandelier catch the light in this already light and airy room. The plain lines of the rest of the room show their intricacy to advantage and they bring a happy touch of whimsy to a room where functionality often ousts other considerations.

index

acknowledgements

Author's acknowledgements

I would like to thank interior designer Debby Thurston for mounting and supplying the sample board on page 36 – she can be contacted at Thurston.assocs@virgin.net and also Dominic Bailey for his editorial research. I would also like to thank my editors Sarah Tomley and Alice Tyler for their hand-holding.

Publisher's acknowledgements

Executive editor Sarah Tomley
Editor Alice Tyler
Executive art editor Karen Sawyer
Design Cobalt ID
Picture researcher Lucia Strohmayer
Senior production controller Ian Paton

Picture acknowledgements

Abode /Tim Imrie 26.

The Alternative Flooring Company /www.alternativeflooring.com (stockists tel: ++44 (0) 1264 335111) product: 'Buckingham Basketware', 'Multi Bouclé Dalkeith', 'Bouclé Broome' 5 right, 79.

Amorim Flooring UK /www.wicanders.com (stockists tel: ++44 (0) 1403 710001) product: 'Elegance Gold Brown Pastel' 72.

BCT Ltd /www.bctltd.co.uk (stockists tel: ++44 (0) 1626 831480) product: 'London Chelsea' 54.

Craven Dunnil & Co Ltd /www.cravendunnill.co.uk (stockists tel: ++44 (0) 1746 761611) product: 'Rennaisance Gold Moresca' 68.

Crown Paint /www.crownpaint.co.uk (stockists tel: ++44 (0) 870 24021127) product: 'Adriatic Crown Solo One Coat Emulsion' 9, 15.

Crown Wallcoverings /www.wallpapers-uk.com (stockists tel: ++44 (0) 01254 222800) product: 'Smart Rooms range' 48.

DIY Photo Library 70.

Dulux /www.dulux.com (stockists tel: ++44 (0) 1753 550555) 34.

Fired Earth Interiors /www.firedearth.com (stockists tel: ++44 (0) 1295 814300) 3, 10 left, 10 right, 27, 52,55, 61, 64, 65, 69 top.

Forbo Flooring /www.marmoleum.co.uk (stockists tel: ++44 (0) 800 7312369) 73.

Graham & Brown Limited /www.grahambrown.com (stockists tel: ++44 (0) 800 3288452) 7, 29, 37, 46 left, 46 centre, 46 right, 47, 51.

International Paints /www.international-paints.co.uk (stockists tel: ++44 (0) 1480 484284) 83, 85, 86, 88, 89, 90, 91, 92, 93, 94, 95, 96, 97, 98, 99, 100, 101, 102, 103.

Octopus Publishing Group Limited 36 /Linda Burgess 18 centre right /Paul Forrester 57 /Sandra Lane 19, 32 /Di Lewis 13 left /Tom Mannion 10 centre, 16, 17, 18 left, 18 right /Neil Mersh 35 /Peter Myers 30, 78 /Pia Tryde 39, 43 /Mark Winwood 18 centre left /Polly Wreford 12, 13 right, 63, 67, 69 bottom /Mel Yates 24.

Ray Main /Mainstream 25, 40, designer: Fleur Rossdale 60, 82.

Original Style Ltd /www.originalstyle.com (stockists tel: ++44 (0) 1392 474058) 56.

Papa Architects Ltd /www.papaarchitects.co.uk (tel: ++44 (0) 20 83488411) 5 left, 11, 14.

Pergo /www.pergo.com (stockists tel: ++44 (0) 800 3742771) product: 'Original Oak Plank' 74.

Reed Harris /www.reedharris.co.uk (stockists tel: ++44 (0) 20 77367511) product: 'White gloss Arte round mosaic' 53.

Rohm & Haas Paint Quality Institute /www.paintquality.co.uk 21, 22, 28, 31, 33, 41.

Stoddard /www.stoddardcarpets.com (stockists tel: ++44 (0) 800 0724888) represented by the Carpet Foundation /www.comebacktocarpet.com 81.